D1093098

PSYCHING IN SPORT

PSYCHING IN SPORT

The psychological preparation for
serious competition in sport

Brent S. Rushall, PH.D

PELHAM BOOKS: LONDON

First published in Great Britain by
Pelham Books Ltd
44 Bedford Square
London W.C.1
1979

ISBN 0 7207 1193 2

Composition by Allset
and printed and bound in Great Britain by
A. Wheaton & Company Limited, Exeter

79 008721

Contents

*Dedicated to the
memory of the late
Thomas William Rushall*

Preface

There has evolved recently a science of superior athletic performance. It has become obvious that the physiologies, biomechanics and psychologies of elite athletes are different to those of athletes who have not achieved world ranking performances. Of concern to this text are those psychological behaviours and stimuli which affect an elite athlete's performance in serious competitions (national championships, etc.). The content of the information that is presented in this volume is derived from two sources, (1) the empirical behaviour information obtained from athletes of international stature, and (2) the findings of researches within the psychology of stress adaptation and coping which have relevance for serious athletic performance.

A basic assumption of this presentation is that there is a model form of athletic preparation. A set of principles of behaviour needs to be followed to produce a maximum sporting performance. This involves the adaptation of a series of procedures and decision-making processes to the particular sport and individual concerned. It is proposed that there are principles of behaviour which need to be adhered to by coaches and athletes alike. These principles are akin to the principles of physiology and biomechanics which must be followed and implemented to produce training outcomes. Another set of principles exists which must be followed to produce competition outcomes. Those principles are the substance of this book.

Since an ideal model is proposed it stands to reason that the handling of young, developing athletes is a designed process which aims to cultivate coping, self-controlled behaviours which are in alignment with known behavioural principles.   Thus, some of the competition and training experiences of maturing athletes are learning events which are designed to develop appropriate, competent behaviours which facilitate maximum performances.   Coaches are required to teach and develop behaviours for competition preparation with the same intent and application as is applied to the development of skilled behaviours and adaptation to physical stress.   As a result of this supposition, there is no singular model of pre-competition control for age-group or inexperienced athletes.   A preparation for an improving athlete contains a series of directed activities which are learning experiences.   The outcome of a series of preparations should be the behavioural competencies and procedures, that is, the ingredients of the model, which are described in the following pages.

Competition preparations for athletes are usually limited in their scope.   Coaches often prescribe stereo-typed behaviours which are not conducive to maximum performances. Others allow athletes to 'experience' freely the situations and trial-and-error adaptations of each competitive circumstance.   Eventually, they become 'experienced' athletes who may or may not follow behavioural patterns which facilitate the best possible athletic performances.   Superstitious behaviours, which are primarily non-functional for athletic performance, are common outcomes of this unstructured 'discovery' method of development.   Other forms of pre-competition control exist but the amazing feature common to these processes is that a small number of athletes survive in spite of what is thrust upon them by the majority of coaches.   The information which is now available can aid coaches and athletes together to develop better forms of pre-competition and competition behaviours.   What will be required, however, is some initiative and innovation in adapting and applying the psychological preparation model to each unique individual, situation and sport.

A need for competition preparation

The scope of this text is limited to the events and actions which occur on the day of competition. A major reason for this concentration is that the day of competition is the single, most important day for affecting performance. The critical influences in that day are psychological. No more training can be done to improve the psychological status of an athlete; no new skills can be learned. On the competition day, an athlete is faced with a finite potential for energy and skill production. There exists a potential for a performance that is limited by physiology and biomechanics. The task of the coach and athlete together is to perform to the upper bounds of those limits. Unfortunately, few athletes are able to perform optimally in a consistent manner in serious competitions. There are many examples of athletes performing exceptionally well in preliminary events and then producing inferior performances in finals. The practising coach often refers to these performance reductions as 'choking', 'psyche-outs', 'quitting', 'freezing', 'stage-fright', etc. The mere fact that an athlete produces a performance of one level in a heat and then fails to produce at least the same standard in the final is reason for great concern. Between the two performances there has been no change in physiological or skill capacity; only psychological factors have altered. It is possible to prevent these performance decrements by controlling the psychological factors which surround competition environments.

In a similar vein, within competitions there are often wide ranges of fluctuations in performance standards. A team can dominate the first half of a contest only to alter its performance competency in the second half and allow the opposition to recover and win. Shifts in dominance are commonly referred to as changes in 'momentum'. The changes are usually not precipitated by physiological factors or by sudden reductions in the limits of skilled abilities. They are usually caused by psychological events.

The present general status of competition control is one of

confusion.   Home-spun philosophies, superstitious behavioural anecdotes, admissions of a lack of appropriate knowledge, neglect, each mixed with some useful and appropriate
procedures, all contribute to widely divergent competition
preparation recipes which result in equally divergent variations
of performance. This text attempts to define the appropriate
forms of athlete control that produce consistent performances
in competition which result in the full utilization of the
physiological and skill potential of the athlete or team.

This claim may be considered to be presumptuous. However, it is no more audacious than some of the types of
behaviours which accompany the preparations of elite
athletes and teams in serious competitions. The hiring of an
astrologer to help in the preparations of the Oakland Athletics baseball team; the open use of a pyramid totem by the
Toronto Mapleleafs' coach Mr Red Kelly as an aid to improving his team's Stanley Cup play-off chances; Mr Kelly's
use of spraying 'negative ions' from an aerosol can the following year for a similar reason; and the consumption of monkey
meat by one team at the World Cup soccer tournament, are
examples of how the outcomes of competitions are entrusted
to superstitious hopes and singular factors rather than empirically verified design principles. That such outrageous
happenings could exist in the circles of elite athletics is a sad
commentary on the status of the science of competition preparation.

A further requirement for a concentration on competition
preparations is produced by the nature of modern sporting
competition itself. The continued improvements in performance which have been brought about by the many advances
in sports training and technologies have led to the requirement for attending to every minute detail and factor that
might affect a sport performance. The athlete development
process is now very involved, detailed and complicated.
With the outcomes of contests often depending solely on one
human action or being measured in microscopic proportions,
factors of minor influence are important. It has been possible

previously for a coach to be less than precise and still aid athletes to achieve in sports competitions. That luxury is no longer available. It is now necessary to implement precisioned procedures to develop elite performances in the majority of sports. One area where precision can be instituted is in competition preparation.

There is a need to emphasize the preparatory procedures for competition. This text focuses on that need.

Psychological preparation as a training emphasis
As the awareness and recognition of psychological preparation and training grows, it becomes obvious that the content of training programs should emphasize psychological training to an extent that at least matches the physiological and skill emphases. The development of psychological skills and capacities is a learning-adaptation process of parallel importance and time requirement as is generally afforded training and skill development. Consequently, the success of the implementation of the control and management model for competition that is proposed here will largely depend upon the developmental process which precedes it. Thus, the production of competition competence is not a short-term or one-shot exposure. Rather, it takes time to develop and to optimize the individual ingredients that are necessary for a maximum performance.

What is required is practice and development through training. The outcome should be both overt and covert behaviours which are planned, predictable and familiar. Thus, it is not only what an athlete does that is important but also what he/she thinks. Training should incorporate methods which teach athletes how to cope, interpret, make decisions and control themselves. These behaviours are the substance of maximized competition preparations.

The scope of this text
In attempting to present the preparation model, a focus will be made on what and how to do the appropriate actions.

Why these actions should be done will be briefly alluded to primarily through the medium of referencing at least one academic work that serves to validate the stated principle or characteristic. The important aspect for coaches and athletes to realize is that knowing why something occurs may be useful but only in a limited way. What is more useful, in fact essential, is knowing what and how to do something so that effects can be achieved. This is emphasized in this text. It will have failed its intent if the reader is not able to apply its directives to actual circumstances.

The scope of this text is limited. It focuses on the short-term, competition day factors which affect performance. Topics such as motivation, skill learning, problem athletes, etc., will not be considered. They remain for discussion in other volumes and sources.

An important distinction is also made with regard to psychology itself. Psychology contains cause and effect principles. It is no longer satisfactory to talk in psychological terms to generate an impression of knowing about psychology. Coaches have previously been able to explain away athletes' and their own deficiencies by using vague psychological terminologies after a performance or behaviour. With the state of psychology being what it is today, individuals charged with the responsibility for controlling behaviour can no longer transfer the responsibility for behaviour failure to the performer or some other source. There now exists a technology for behaviour control. This technology is appropriate for competition preparation. Failure to control performances in competitions constitutes a coaching failure. Now it is the responsibility of a coach to monitor, describe and evaluate what he/she does to produce changes and to control psychological factors in athletic performances. This text describes those control features and psychological principles. In doing this the operations for causing behaviour changes are described and limited to realistic bounds. The emphasis on realism is assumed. The days of coaching and performing through hope are no longer appropriate. Coaches and athletes alike must be realistic when interpreting the competitive circumstance to be able to cope and to control behaviour in a predictable way.

The stress of this text on the individual is deliberate. There are many individual sports which require such an obvious concentration. However, this emphasis is no less important for team sports which have been shown to be a collection of individuals rather than a massed psyche. The task of preparing teams for competition is usually more difficult than it is for individual events primarily because of the logistics involved. In proposing this point, a distinction is made among coaching strategies. It is easier and more commonly observed that coaches treat all athletes in a similar fashion. A group orientation and universal handling strategy is used. Admittedly, such a strategy is facilitative and expedient for the coach. Because it is easy and simple does not mean that it is the best method. The principle of individual differences is paramount when coaching elite athletes. It is only when an individual's strengths are maximized and the weaknesses minimized that an athlete has a chance of achieving the true potential of a performance. Clearly, this achievement is not attained when a singular handling strategy is applied to a group of athletes. For coaches of teams and large squads, methods for individualizing preparatory procedures will have to be devised. Some possibilities will be described in the following pages.

A final limitation to the scope of this text is that for an elite athlete to function effectively his/her control and management must be self-directed. Thus, *it concentrates on what the athlete can do for him/herself prior to competition.* This contrasts with the often displayed coaching behaviour of the coach orchestrating an athlete's preparation. The production of coach-reliant activities does not facilitate maximum performances. It is contrary to the actions evidenced in elite athletes prior to and during competitions. The role of the coach should be to develop behaviours in athletes to the extent that preparation decisions and actions are self-determined.

This book concentrates on the causal factors and preparatory behaviours and thoughts which affect the standard of an athletic performance. The items considered are those which exist on the day of performance. The important information that is presented is what and how things should be done in the preparatory process. A general model for developing individual, self-controlled behaviours is described. In applying the model the individual athlete and coach together work to individualize the content so that performance preparations are controlled, planned and predictable. The scope of the preparations is primarily psychological.

Finally, the main principles and content of this text were developed from and included in the Level III Theory Manual of the National Coaching Certification Program of the Coaching Association of Canada. This book extends the ideas, references, and practical applications of those writings. The cooperation of the Coaching Association of Canada in allowing the duplication of some content is gratefully acknowledged.

Thunder Bay,   Brent S. Rushall
Ontario

1   Elite Athletes at Competitions

It is possible to hypothesize what are the appropriate pre-competition and competition behaviours of high level athletes which facilitate their performance of superior feats. In the past, academic guesses of this type have often proved to be incomplete, inaccurate and uninformed. The fact that elite athletes do produce superior performances and with relative consistency indicates that the majority of them must be doing some things correctly. It is expedient and accurate to learn from these individuals and to develop valid and reliable information from their revelations. It stands to reason that not all athletes will be behaving correctly all of the time. However, most of them will have appropriate behaviours most of the time. It is worthwhile to see what are the pre-competition and competition behaviours and character-istics that are displayed by the majority of elite athletes. If there are consistent sets of events and actions which exist it should be possible to amalgamate this information with the research of similar scope and thus develop a detailed, valid model of superior pre-competition and competition practices.

OBTAINING INFORMATION
Over the past five years sport-specific psychological inven-tories have been developed (Rushall 1978a). These tests have concentrated on behaviours, situations and characteristics of sports and their participants. They have avoided the use of psychological constructs, such as determination, coach-ability, reactivity, etc., which are purely descriptive and vague, and have little utility for predicting specific situational

behaviours which are the focus of coaching. One section of most of the sport-specific inventories concentrates on evaluating pre-competition and competition behaviours. By looking at the results of the questions concerning these two areas it is possible to 'understand' what elite athletes do and think in competition related circumstances.

SOME ELITE ATHLETES

Tables 1 and 2 list the responses of ten groups of elite athletes to questions about pre-competition and competition behaviours. These athletes are world ranked and clearly superior in their performances and capabilities. The groups are:

1   The starters of the 1976 USA Men's Volleyball Team that competed at the Montreal Olympic Games.
2   The ten 1976 Canadian Olympic Games Freestyle Wrestling Team members.
3   Those 1976 Canadian Olympic Games Swimming Team members who were Olympic finalists (men and women).
4   The members of the 1978 Canadian Commonwealth Games Men's Swimming Team who were Games' medallists.
5   The members of the 1978 Canadian Commonwealth Games Women's Swimming Team who were Games' medallists.
6   The starting five men of the 1978 Canadian Men's Basketball Team.
7   Three female world-ranked 1976 Canadian Olympic divers.
8   The three top 1976 Canadian women skiers.
9   Twelve members of the 1977 Canadian Men's Lightweight Rowing crews.
10   Seventeen swimmers who have held world records or won world championship medals since 1973 (men and women).

These athletes are not representative of all sports. There is a predominance of swimmers and only two team sports, volleyball and basketball, included. This raises the spectre of the commonalities between these groups being biassed and not being indicative of most sports. This doubt is alleviated if the number of common features between the ten groups is high and consistent. The entries in the two tables are indicated as being present in an athletic group if the majority of group members indicated the behaviour or characteristic specified when they originally completed the tests. When the majority of the groups indicated a behaviour or characteristic it could be considered a universal feature. In some situations less than a majority also indicated important information.

When considering these features several things should be remembered. First, if the results of this survey are in accordance with the findings of independent psychological researches then there is a strong argument for them being 'universal' features. Second, if there is a fairly complete set of commonalities across all the behaviours and characteristics for all the groups, then there is also a strong argument for sport pre-competition and competition conduct. Finally, since the majority of the athletic groups are Canadian there is a possibility of these data only being valid for Canadians. However, the USA Volleyball Team and 14 of the 17 'world' swimmers were not Canadian so when they indicate features they validate extending the findings beyond Canadians. This extension is further strengthened when psychological research supports the item in question. Admittedly, this study is limited but it is valuable for suggesting possible elite athlete behaviours which can be 'cross-validated' through the findings of scholarly research.

A final feature should be understood about these subjects. There has been no discrimination based on sex. This is because pre-competition and competition behaviours do not discriminate the sex of the athlete. Other sporting behaviours and behavioural characteristics do. Hence, for competition preparations it is appropriate to apply these same principles of development and control to all athletes, whether they be male or female.

BEHAVIOURAL CHARACTERISTICS OF ELITE ATHLETES
Tables 1 and 2 list thirty-six specific features which have
been reliably evaluated through testing elite athletes. Each of
these will be considered below with comments and qualifi-
cations made where appropriate. Table 1 enumerates pre-
competition behaviours and Table 2 indicates competition
behaviours.

Pre-competition Behaviours and Characteristics
  1. *More effort and intensity is put into competition than
into training.* Eight of the ten groups indicated this characteristic. These athletes are able to discern that they have
something 'extra' which can be used in competitive circumstances. This suggests a reasonable justification for expecting
elite athletes to produce a competition performance that is
better than those achieved while in training or lesser competitions. It is a relevant feature to be considered when setting
performance goals for serious competitions.
  2. *The more detailed a competition plan, the more confident the athlete feels.* This was indicated by a majority of
the groups. It suggests that competition plans should be
specific and detailed possibly to a point of definition that is
not commonly considered by coaches. The fact that this
action also is considered to enhance confidence is important.
  3. *A contest plan which tells the athlete what to do if
things do not go as expected is needed.* This means that the
athletes appreciate being able to cope with and adapt to
unusual or unexpected situations which arise in competition.
Thus, not only does an athlete have a primary plan of action
but also a secondary set of alternatives that can be employed
if needed.
  4. *Being alone before a competition is preferred.* This
characteristic is evidenced by athletes in individual sports.
  5. *Warming-up by him/herself is preferred.* The actual
activity of warm-up appears to be an individual activity. The
basketball players indicated this but the volleyball players
did not. This difference is understandable because the warm-

up activities of volleyball cannot be adequately performed without a partner, whereas in basketball they can. Rowers have to be with other crew members. With divers, because of limited facilities, it is an accepted fact that warm-ups are taken in turn in the presence of other competitors. What is suggested here is that where it is possible, warm-up activities are completed independently of other athletes.

6. *Warm-ups contain practices of things to be done in competition.*   All groups of athletes indicated that they practised activities which were to be used in the competition.

7. *Need for a coach during warm-ups.*   The need or no need for a coach to assist athletes during warm-ups is not clearly indicated.   What is suggested in these data is that athletes like coaches to be present during warm-ups and prefer to use the coach as a resource if needed. This contrasts to the coaching concept of the coach being important and necessary for warm-ups.   There is a possibility that coaches could interfere with an athlete's preparation if he/she were to push him/herself into the warm-up activities in functions that were deemed to be unnecessary by the athlete.

8. *Not worrying about other competitors before a contest.*   Half the groups indicated that they did not worry about other competitors before a contest.   This is not possible before a combative sport such as wrestling.   A competition strategy for wrestling is partly based upon scouting reports of opponents.   In team games a similar attempt to scout and exploit opponent weaknesses requires a consideration of opponents.   The major feature to be realized here is whether opponents are objectively considered or the athlete worries about them.   In non-interactive contests it usually is not necessary to concentrate on opponents.   Most successful competitors do not get preoccupied with contemplating their opponents.   Any form of consideration should not be to the detriment of focusing attention on the approaching task.

9. *Nervous and tense.*   Being nervous and tense is a sympton of arousal. High levels of arousal that are controlled

can be translated into high levels of performance. In some sports the level of tension and nervousness should not be as high as in other activities. What is surprising about some of these groups is that competitions do not produce states of arousal (tension and nervousness) which differ from those experienced in other circumstances.

10. *If troubled before a contest he/she knows what to do to regain composure.* All groups indicated the capacity to regain composure if required. This is an index of self-control.

11. *If too excited before a contest he/she knows what to do to calm down.* This self-control indication suggests that elite athletes are able to monitor and control their own levels of arousal. It also suggests that they have some awareness of a 'desirable' level of arousal, that which it is intended to achieve during a competition preparation.

12. *If confidence is lost before a contest he/she knows what to do to recover it.* An athlete's confidence would appear to be a feature which needs to be controlled. Thoughts and behaviours which are incompatible with confidence are detrimental to performance (Wine 1971). Confidence has been found to be a significant psychological discriminator between successful and unsuccessful wrestlers contending for international team selections (Highlen & Bennett 1978). The ability to regain or control confidence would be an advantage as it would be a means of eliminating one potential source of performance variation.

13. *As many mental rehearsals as possible are undertaken before a competition.* This item coincides with feature number 6 indicating a focus of attention on the forthcoming performance.

14. *An ability to concentrate totally on an approaching contest throughout the whole preparatory period.* This characteristic further strengthens the concept of a singular focus of attention on the ensuing performance.

15. *An assessment of being a good judge of how well he/she will do in competition.* This indicates a knowledge about oneself with regard to current athletic status and its relevance

to performance. The important feature here is an element of self-awareness.

16. *Always being confident that he/she can perform to expectations in competition.* This has been mentioned in item number 12. However, it is surprising that only half of the groups indicated this confidence level.

17. *Being able to handle unusual circumstances at competitions.* Sudden changes or distractions prior to or during competitions are not likely to alter the singular, positive approach to competition of these athletes.

18. *Unfamiliar competition arenas do not affect performances.*

19. *Not being upset by small distractions or problems which occur before important competitions.* This is a further feature of the coping capacity for handling the varieties of stressors which occur prior to competitions.

The previous 19 items indicate several decided behaviours and characteristics that show what an elite athlete should be doing while preparing for competitions. Elite athletes consider that they have something extra above that which has been expended in training, which can be released in competition to increase the intensity and effort of application. Competitions are planned in detail. The detail includes coping behaviours which can be used to adapt to unusual or unexpected circumstances. The practices of warm-up are self-focused and, where possible, carried out alone. The content of a warm-up is focused both physically and mentally on the anticipated activities of the forthcoming competition. Elite athletes suggest an awareness of the feelings and sensations which are necessary to produce a good performance. Consequently, if there are changes in levels of excitedness or confidence these athletes can readjust to the appropriate level. They have the capacities to effect these behavioural modifications. They also have the coping behaviours which enable them to adjust to upsetting circumstances and distractions which occur in the pre-competition period. The

TABLE 1

Pre-competition Behaviours and Characteristics of 10 Groups of Elite Athletes.[a]

Characteristics	Groups[b]									
	USA Volleyball (M)	Can. Wrestlers (M)	1976 Can. Swimmers	1978 Swimmers (M)	1978 Swimmers (F)	Can. Basketball (M)	Can. Divers (F)	Can. Skiers (F)	Can. Rowers (M)	World Swimmers
1. More effort and intensity is put into competition than into training.	✓	—	✓	✓	✓	✓	✓	—	✓	✓
2. The more detailed the competition plan, the more confident the athlete feels.	—	✓	✓	✓	✓	✓	—	✓	✓	✓
3. A contest plan which tells the athlete what to do if things do not go as expected is needed.	—	✓	✓	✓	✓	✓	—	✓	✓	✓
4. Being alone before a competition is preferred.	—	✓	✓	✓	✓	—	—	✓	—	✓
5. Warming-up by him/herself is preferred.	—	✓	✓	✓	✓	✓	—	✓	—	✓
6. Warm-ups contain practices of things to be done in competition.	✓	✓	✓	✓	✓	✓	✓	✓	✓	✓

7. Need for a coach during warm-ups.
   No need for a coach during warm-ups.
8. Not worrying about other competitors before a contest.
9. Nervous and tense.
10. If troubled before a contest he/she knows what to do to regain composure.
11. If too excited before a contest he/she knows what to do to calm down.
12. If confidence is lost before a contest he/she knows what to do to recover it.
13. As many mental rehearsals as possible are undertaken before a competition.
14. An ability to concentrate totally on an approaching contest throughout the whole preparatory period.
15. Being a good judge of how well he/she will do in a contest.
16. Always being confident that he/she can perform to expectations in competition.
17. Being able to handle unusual circumstances at competitions.
18. Unfamiliar competition arenas do not affect performance.
19. Not being upset by small distractions or problems which occur before important competitions.

a Descriptions of groups are in the text   b — = absent; √ = present; N = not applicable pre-competition period features a self-oriented focus of attention that is totally aimed at the ensuing performance. Pre-competition events which occur will not disrupt this preoccupation to the point where the following competitive performance will suffer.

Competition Behaviours and Characteristics

1. *A preference for taking an early lead no matter how much effort is required.* The swimming groups did not evidence this characteristic. This is probably because that sport is very dependent upon individual pacing plans aimed at achieving a maximum performance. 'Going out too fast' can be very detrimental to swimming performances. In skiing, this characteristic is not appropriate because there is no head-to-head competition, all events being completed on a maximum effort time-trial basis. For those sports where it is applicable, elite athletes attempt to establish superiority as soon as possible without concern for the latter parts of the contest.

2. *If not selected to start a game he/she will be ready and fully prepared to go into the game at any time.* This is appropriate for team-substitution games. Only the volleyball team indicated this feature.

3. *A preference to play his/her own game/race/match and regulate his/her own effort levels.* Only half the groups indicated this characteristic. Intuitively, one would have expected this to be a common quality amongst elite athletes as it would be the outcome of the detailed plans and the focus of attention that were features of the pre-competition behaviours.

4. *In contests there is no saving oneself in order to make a good finishing effort.* This feature suggests that elite athletes need to assert themselves early in a contest. They are not hesitant to achieve an immediate in-performance goal. This characteristic is aligned with feature number 1.

5. *When tired, concentration is on technique.* Swimmers indicated this feature. It constitutes a method of distracting

the athlete from the sensations of fatigue.

6. *When tiredness starts to be felt these athletes try harder.*

7. *These athletes exert maximum efforts even if they know that they cannot improve their situation.* Competition goals include self-evaluations as well as contest outcomes. If a positive contest outcome cannot be achieved, the self-oriented goals are sufficiently strong to warrant making the competitive effort maximal.

8. *If these athletes fall behind they still make the contest a test to see if they can perform a best effort.* This validates the strength of self-evaluation goals for the competitive efforts of elite athletes.

9. *The punishing aspects of the sport do not distract these athletes' applications to contests.*

10. *These athletes will continue competing even if injured.* This characteristic is appropriate for sports where gross measures of performance are used and the consequences of the injury may not be drastic. For precise sports, such as swimming and skiing where performances are measured to thousandths of a second and the competitions are usually very close, it often is not worth competing with the handicap of an injury.

11. *No matter how difficult the play, these athletes will try for the ball rather than let it go.* Both volleyball and basketball players indicated this feature. It suggests a willingness never to give up on any point.

12. *Poor calls or biassed refereeing do not upset these athletes' performances.*

13. *These athletes want time-outs to be used profitably and constructively.* Game or contest interruptions should be used to focus attention on the game or match and to provide information which can be used to improve the contest status.

14. *These athletes can handle the pressure in the final stages of a close contest.* This is an index of confidence that elite athletes have in their own abilities.

15. *An ability to concentrate on aspects of a strategy throughout the whole contest.* The focus of attention is the

TABLE 2

Competition Behaviours and Characteristics of 10 Groups of Elite Athletes.[a]

Characteristics	Groups[b]									
	USA Volleyball (M)	Can. Wrestlers (M)	1976 Can. Swimmers	1978 Swimmers (M)	1978 Swimmers (F)	Can. Basketball (M)	Can. Divers (F)	Can. Skiers (F)	Can. Rowers (M)	World Swimmers
1. A preference for taking an early lead no matter how much effort is required.	√	√	—	—	—	√	√	—	√	—
2. If not selected to start a game he/she will be ready and fully prepared to go into the game at any time.	√	N	N	N	N	—	N	N	N	N
3. A preference to play his/her own game/race/match and regulate his/her own effort levels.	√	—	—	√	√	—	—	—	√	√
4. In contests there is no saving oneself in order to make a good finishing effort.	√	√	—	—	—	—	√	—	√	√
5. When tired, concentration is on technique.	—	—	√	√	√	√	—	√	—	√
6. When tiredness starts to be felt these athletes try harder.	√	√	√	√	√	√	—	—	√	√

7. These athletes exert maximum efforts even if they know they cannot improve their situation.	✓	✓	✓	✓	✓	✓	—	✓
8. If these athletes fall behind they still make the contest a test to see if they can perform a best effort.	✓	✓	✓	✓	✓	✓	—	✓
9. The punishing aspects of the sport do not distract these athletes' applications to contests.	✓	N	N	✓	N	N	N	N
10. These athletes will continue competing even if injured.	—	✓	—	—	—	✓	—	—
11. No matter how difficult the play, these athletes will try for the ball rather than let it go.	✓	N	N	✓	N	N	N	N
12. Poor calls or biassed refereeing do not upset these athletes' performance.	✓	✓	N	✓	N	N	N	N
13. These athletes want time-outs to be used profitably and constructively.	✓	✓	N	✓	N	—	N	N
14. These athletes can handle the pressure in the final stages of a close contest.	✓	✓	✓	✓	✓	—	✓	✓
15. An ability to concentrate on aspects of a strategy throughout the whole contest.	✓	✓	—	—	—	—	✓	✓
16. Information and experiences gained in a contest are used to modify strategies for the next contest.	✓	✓	—	✓	—	—	✓	✓

[a]Descriptions of the groups are in the text   [b]— = absent; ✓ = present; N = not applicable.

performance and characteristics of the performance. Unrelated items which are not task-specific are not contemplated.

16. *Information and experiences gained in a contest are used to modify strategies for the next contest.* Each competitive effort is a learning experience which provides feedback for better planning of the next contest. De-briefing sessions and self-evaluations are two forms of formalizing this action.

These competition characteristics suggest a variety of competition features which are pre-planned and structured. There is a need to assert the level of effort immediately to the point of either advancing ahead of opponents or establishing oneself on a task completion strategy. Little regard is given to the costs of establishing this dominance. Plans and strategies are considered and maintained throughout a performance in spite of distractions such as poor officiating, substitutions, etc. The majority of athletes perform in spite of injury and fatigue. The onset of fatigue is a stimulus to increase the level of effort. During the performance, a concentration on task-specific factors is developed. These athletes reflect upon their performances and through evaluation attempt to influence their next performance by modifying their plans accordingly.

THE MEANING OF DESCRIPTIONS
It is a worthwhile venture to contemplate the meaning of the above descriptions. It is important to point out that the discussed descriptions are far from complete. They have been limited to the content of restricted questions on standardized psychological tests. Because of this restriction not all the questions about pre-competition and competition behaviours may have been asked. It should be conceivable to expand this empirically gained knowledge by considering the psychological research that is available. Thus, it should be possible to embellish these known qualities. The descriptions that have been presented here are also generalized. Consequently, they may not describe individuals exactly. A

more appropriate form of consideration for these stereo-typed descriptions is to contemplate them as being core be-haviours which need to be appended with further behaviours that are peculiar to an individual. This should develop the best pre-competition and competition preparations for the individual athlete. This should also result in various adapta-tions of the sound central core set of behaviours that produce elite types of competitive performance behaviours.

A third consideration is also warranted. The possibility that the behaviours exhibited by elite athletes today may not yet be optimal is very real. Past sporting histories have shown that what is done today more than likely will not be appro-priate in the future. Thus, it remains the responsibility of coaches, athletes, and in particular sport scientists, to antici-pate the future changes in sport performance preparations and develop athletes according to well-reasoned predictions. Thus, the meshing of the characteristics which have been discussed plus the findings developed within the laboratory, which usually precede a more general acceptance and 'normal' use, will generate an even better form of athlete preparation for competition than that which is presently in use.

To aid the coach to evaluate an athlete for pre-competition and competition behaviours and characteristics a standard-ized questionnaire is included in appendix A. That test is similar to those contained in the inventories which were used to generate the above descriptions.

The following chapters consider the sources of problems which arise during the preparatory procedures for serious competitions. These problems will be considered and sug-gested solutions described. A successful implementation procedure will also be discussed. What is required of the reader is a constant evaluation of the concepts and limited examples which are presented. One of the restraints of this book is that only a restricted number of examples is allowed. Compounding this confinement is the fact that athlete preparations of a deliberate nature are used today only on a limited basis. Hence, the real examples which can be presented are also restricted. For readers who are not involved with the exampled sports, there is a need to exercise initiative by analogizing the sampled situations to their own sport and then inventing the steps which will make it feasible to produce better forms of competition preparation and conduct in that sport.

2 Potential Problem Areas at Competitions

With any individual preparing for or performing in competition there are a large number of factors which can affect the outcome and style of performance. It is wise to consider that each person's competition effort is affected more by a unique combination of factors which are common to a number of athletes. The higher the level of performance expected of an athlete the more important are these individual factors. It should be stressed, then, that a coach will need to develop a skill for interpreting and recognizing the sets of individual factors which are likely to influence an athlete's performance. This applies equally as well to individuals who constitute a team.

However, it is also a requirement for effective coaching that a coach should be aware of the potential problem areas which could arise that might detract from an athlete's performance. If these sources of influence are known then a coach should be able to train individual athletes to be able to recognize them and to cope with them in a positive and constructive manner. Thus, a coach will need to know all the possible sources of performance debilitating factors and to make his/her athletes aware of those which are influential for each individual.

In a general discussion it is not possible to list every potential problem area. It is possible to indicate some universal problems that could occur in every sporting situation. Some of these will be discussed below. It will remain for coaches to add to these general factors those items and events which are peculiar to their sports and to the athletes under their care.

INCREASED ANXIETY

As a competition approaches there should be an increase in an athlete's readiness to perform. This increase is usually manifested as heightened levels of activity. This activity includes increased physiological arousal (the General Activation Syndrome—GAS) and increased mental activity. The content of mental activity is important. It controls the readiness to perform. The physiological arousal governs the intensity of effort in the competitive activity if it is accompanied by the appropriate thought patterns.

Athletes vary greatly in the time period in which the arousal increase occurs. Some elite athletes exhibit heightened arousal as much as two weeks before an important competition. Others may not exhibit indications of changes in arousal until several hours before an event. The length of time is unique for each athlete. Because of this individuality, it stands to reason that those athletes who experience very early changes in arousal will be more susceptible to detrimental factors. They simply have more time for them to be influential. Consequently, the early arousal athletes may be more problematical than those who are late in being aroused. This extra time will require a greater amount of vigilant control but it will not result in any more complicated procedures.

A person's preparedness to act is determined by both physical activation (arousal) and mental activation (Firth 1973). A distinction should be made between arousal itself (GAS) and arousal-based emotion. The latter is a result of arousal plus a context that provides cues for appropriately labelling the arousal. It is a mix of appropriate mental and physical readiness and is often called primary emotion (Harris & Katkin 1975). This is what is desirable for an athlete to achieve in the pre-competition period.

Performance problems occur with secondary emotions.

When emotional behaviours are developed through thought processes alone, and produce a physiological arousal even though the emotional state is not dependent upon it, inappropriate mental and physical activity can occur. Similarly, when an appropriate level of arousal exists, but is accompanied by an inappropriate pattern of mental activity, performances are affected. It is important that the mental activity which precedes competitions is controlled to the extent both of its being limited to the ensuing task requirements, and to its being in harmony with the state of arousal. The major secondary emotion which causes problems is anxiety.

If athletes become *anxious* during the preparatory period before performance then the ensuing effort is very likely to be of a lower standard than should be expected (Bobey & Davidson 1970). Anxiety in sports usually results in uncontrolled arousal. The occurrence of anxiety takes many forms, but it is primarily controlled by an athlete's thoughts and appraisals of the impending competitive situation. What is of importance for discussion in this section are the types of thoughts which can cause a performance to be reduced.

There are three classes of thoughts which are of concern. They are: (1) irrelevant thoughts, (2) self-oriented thoughts, and (3) task-oriented thoughts. With respect to anxiety, it is the self-oriented thoughts which cause the problem.

Self-oriented thoughts are characterized by a preoccupation with the athlete's welfare and feelings rather than being more attendant to task-relevant variables. The best description of these thoughts is 'worry'. There is an emphasis on what does not feel right, very minor aches or pains (which could be imaginary), concerns for irrelevant feelings, possible problems with equipment or own bodily functions, etc. The anticipation of negative outcomes and failures to adapt appropriately in the performance are often expressed. The central features of anxiety are the limited scope of orientation (the athlete him/herself and not others, or the impending task), the negative connotations given to events, and fears about immediate future happenings. Highly anxious individuals exhibit a number of performance characteristics, as listed here.

1. They have a reduced ability to use cues which occur in the environment (Easterbrook 1959) and thus, produce an increased number of errors of omission (e.g., 'I didn't see it'; 'I didn't know'; 'Did that happen?'). Simple procedures that the coach may consider to be taken for granted are often neglected.

2. The expression and thinking of anxiety-worry words elicit stress reactions which are usually non-functional (e.g., the athlete does something which has little purpose or relevance to the occasion; there are heightened frequencies and quantities of elimination, such as vomiting, urination, diarrhea; strange physical aches and pains develop).

3. The tolerance of pain and frustration is reduced. Consequently, defeatist attitudes and negative performance predictions are commonly manifested. The quitting point when the task becomes difficult is lowered.

4. Performance errors are over-emphasized and interpreted as being more severe than may be justly warranted. Withdrawal, tantrums, weeping and passive immobilization are symptoms of anxiety which arise when the ensuing task or task-related events are negatively appraised.

It has been shown that worry and heightened anxiety have a greater effect on performance than does an inappropriate physiological state of arousal (Wine 1971). This is a feature which has not been fully appreciated. Athletes who are highly skilled and well-trained can revert to very poor levels of performance purely because of their thought content even though their physiological arousal is at an appropriate level. This detrimental effect can be generated by very short periods of anxiety. It is possible that events or games can be lost in the final few minutes which precede performing because of this phenomenon.

Highly anxious persons are more likely to be distracted by the environment (Wine 1971). If the distractions are irrevelant then the performance will be debilitated even more.

There are procedures which can be invoked to eliminate anxiety and self-oriented thoughts, listed here.

1. Concentration on external events and task-oriented factors.
2. Relaxation sessions incorporating positive mental imagery.
3. The practice of the mental content of performance prior to competition.
4. The recitation and ritualization of behaviours and thoughts before performing.
5. The production of anxiety-incompatible behaviours, thoughts and procedures as pre-competition regimens.

These topics will be discussed in detail in following chapters.

Athletes can learn to behave and think in ways which will not allow anxiety to interfere with performances. There should be no division of attention between self-oriented and task-relevant variables. A concentration on task-relevant variables facilitates superior performances.

CONTROLLED AROUSAL

A characteristic of elite athletes is their ability to control their arousal levels prior to competition (Barry 1979; Fenz & Jones 1972; Genov 1970a). This control leads them to produce appropriate levels of arousal for various levels of standards of performance (Barry 1979; Fiorini 1978; Rushall 1977a). Examples of response and over- and under-exaggeration are rarely seen. Another feature of this control is that elite athletes are aware of the different sensations and feelings that accompany the varying levels of arousal and their relationships to the consequent level of performance. This suggests that heightened self-awareness is a factor involved with arousal control (Barry 1979; Rushall 1977a).

Levels of arousal are controlled by elite athletes prior to

and upon entering competition. Sudden shifts in amounts of arousal are rarely displayed. This phenomenon is just one factor that is involved with producing predictable, familiar behaviours and experiences prior to and during competitions. An ingredient of this stable control is either the inhibition or denial of fears and anxiety. The mental features of pre-competition arousal have to be controlled before effective psychological control can be achieved (Fenz & Jones 1972).

Stable approaches to competition which feature appropriate levels of arousal are developed by:

1. making athletes aware of how they feel prior to competition;
2. trying to recapture feelings and behaviours which have previously occurred prior to good, above average, or outstanding performances; and
3. developing consistent, predictable methods of competition preparation over a period of time.

The procedures for achieving these purposes will be discussed in the following chapters.

Since arousal control is a characteristic of the superior performer, it normally develops through a trial-and-error process that is commonly called 'experience'. There exists the potential for coaches to develop practice sessions and situations which heighten an athlete's awareness of him/herself to accelerate the development of this control process. A failure to control arousal levels will contribute to varying performances in competition. The process for measuring and achieving control will be discussed in the next chapter.

LACK OF ATTENTIONAL CONTROL

Task-oriented thought patterns are necessary to produce maximum performances. The intrusion of self-oriented thoughts has already been discussed as one avenue for decreasing the amount of attention paid to the task to be completed. A variety of distractions also serve to reduce an athlete's ability to control the attention required for optimal performance. Many of these distractions do not have anything to do with performance. Generally, these distractions produce many situations which are commonly referred to as 'psyche-outs'.

The following sub-topics constitute an attempt to categorize the more general debilitating influences which occur within the competition situation.

Non-verbal Cues
Unusual behaviours by competitors, sudden innovations or changes in regimes by others, posturing, the wearing of new uniforms, the actions of other athletes' coaches or support staff members, among many other circumstances, produce thought intrusions which distract from the task at hand. Individuals react to many different events. When unusual circumstances are recognized publicly, for example: the coach criticizes those officiating, or an athlete complains about the accommodation, there is a tendency for these problems to become problems for a group. It is becoming more common now at the national and international levels of competition, that athletes and teams deliberately construct and invoke distractions to affect the performances of other competitors. Although this is an accepted form of activity in North America it is not usual for other nations. At the 1978 Commonwealth Games' swimming events in Edmonton, the concerted efforts of the Canadian Swimming Teams to generate team identification and commitment through structured and timely cheering did distract athletes and visitors from other nations. At the World Aquatic Championships in West Berlin in 1978 a number of nations exhibited deliberate team response and identification activities of the form similar to those common in North America.

Performance Expectation Changes
As part of a consistent approach to performance preparation athletes incorporate one or more performance goals as competition targets. If the frame of reference for the goals or the athlete's perceptions of them is suddenly altered then an

unnecessary distraction is produced. A sudden change in goal orientations reduces an athlete's certainty about attaining a goal. This uncertainty increases the likelihood of 'worry' thoughts occurring. For example, if athletes are getting ready for a track event and one of the favoured competitors starts talking out loud about trying to break a world record in the event, less confident athletes usually will be 'psyched-out' before the contest is begun. This is because they will be expected to upgrade their own performance level further than was planned and will not have time to become accustomed to the new expectation. If this does not occur, then others may concede that the other athlete's expectation of a record as being unattainable for them and thus, they will be defeated before they even start (Schulman 1972). 'Talking big' in this fashion is only effective if it comes from an individual who has the reputation or stature to accompany the boast or statement content. If the boast comes from someone without the credibility to justify it then it will most probably not work. There are many ploys involved in this process of altering performance expectations. Another is to get the opposition to underrrate the competitor's performance expectations. Thus, one hears of athletes 'not trying to win' when in reality they are trying as hard as possible; dissension and fights within a team that are publicized, and usually overblown or sensationalized; these are often ploys to produce overconfidence in or a downgrading of their own performance goals by the opposition (Whiting 1969). O'hara (1977) reported that individuals who experienced a strong awareness of thinking about how others were evaluating them performed poorest. This is analogous to these 'attention getting' and 'attention altering' procedures.

In team situations, idle boasts, expressed doubts, etc., by some team members have the potential to affect the performances of their own team members through the process of vicarious learning (Rushall & Siedentop 1972). In close knit situations like these the coach has to warn athletes as to what type of things can and cannot be said aloud.

Thus, suddenly increased performance expectations or underestimations of opponent abilities without time to adapt to the changes produce inappropriate states of uncertainty or certainty about performance outcomes which will interfere with an athlete's correct attention to the approaching performance. Some psychological models of the interplay of performance expectations between individuals and their effects on interpretations are presented by Pollard and Mitchell (1972).

Outside Distractors

There are many persons that frequent competitive sport environments who unknowingly can distract an athlete from concentrating on a forthcoming performance. They include coaches who offer well-meaning encouragement, well-wishers, parents and other athletes. Generally, they all have the best of intentions but often have the most undesirable effects. Two further major sources of distraction are the press, who could alter an athlete's attention to irrelevant cues or change performance expectations, and crowds or audiences. Apart from being distractions which interrupt the flow and singular purpose of thought control these latter two sources also have the potential to produce negative or anxiety producing aspects of thought. The Canadian Swimming Teams of 1978 were supplied with a booklet entitled 'Meet the Press' that was constructed by this writer. The purpose behind this item was to cue the athletes to appropriate answers to difficult questions which are asked frequently by the press and serve as debilitating distractors. Table 3 lists the questions contained in this booklet. This was an attempt to minimize the effects of press interviews which had been a source of problems in the 1976 Olympic Games in Canada. Audiences and hometown crowds have been commonly documented as having actions and game reactions which affect performers.

Table 3 overleaf

TABLE 3

The List of Questions Contained in the Booklet *Meet the Press*.

1. Do you think that you will win tonight?
2. Will you swim on to the 1980 Olympics?
3. What advice did the coach give you before the race?
4. Who do you think is your main opposition?
5. How did you feel when you knew you were losing the race?
6. How did you feel when you knew you were winning the race?
7. Who were you swimming for?
8. Do you think that all the work you have done was worth it?
9. Are you disappointed in your performance?
10. How will you perform in the Games/Championships?
11. How will Canada fare in the Games/Championships?
12. Has anything gone wrong in your preparation?
13. Are you where you want to be in your training?
14. How tough will the USA/Australia/DDR be?
15. How will you go against so-and-so (Individual)?
16. How was the camp this time compared to that which you had before the '76 Olympics?
17. Do you think that Canadian swimming lacks some things that other countries have?
18. Do you think that the financial support that you receive should be more?
19. What do you think of Canadian sport in general?
20. Why do you think you swam poorly?
21. Are you unhappy that you did not win?

Environment Non-task Factors

There are a host of distractions which are peculiar to only one situation. These are those events which rarely arise and may be characteristic of only one particular environment. These factors might include 'home-town pressures' (unusually severe expectations for performance placed on athletes who reside in the city hosting the event), the presence of other performers or teams who are highly reputed (world champions, record holders, etc.), and factors within the facility which change performance expectations, for example, high jumpers in Mexico City should jump close to their best because of reduced gravity; a tennis player should do better in competition because the playing surface has been changed from grass to hard-court, etc.. Added to those examples are the many incidental happenings which can upset concentration or produce distractions. Some of these are changes of room assignments and facilities, travel disruptions, eating and sleeping arrangements. Competition venues, facilities, organization for the contest, and peculiarities of the situation should be investigated prior to the athletes' exposure to the situation.

There are a number of methods that can be employed to reduce the incidence of events which could interrupt or alter attentional control. One is to shield the athletes from distractions by secluding them in a carefully controlled situation. This is a common practice of East European teams but it is only suitable for short term programs or singular, very important competitions. A more adaptive procedure is the attempt to predict distractions and to teach athletes how to cope with them. Mock press interviews with suggested questions and answers, open discussion of problems that have been experienced by team members and ways of coping with them, and deliberate simulations of competitive environments are some examples of attempts to produce a resilience to being distracted. The initiative and inventiveness of the coach and/or coaching staff is challenged to develop procedures which will develop in athletes a capacity to maintain attentional control in spite of the unique distractors which accompany every competition. The gradual development of these coping capacities will minimize the effects of distractors at further competitions.

HABITUAL THOUGHTS
Some athletes develop habitual thought patterns prior to competition which contain many of the distracting elements which have been discussed above. For example, if an athlete or team has experienced a succession of negative performance

outcomes, there arises the possibility that these negative appraisals will generalize and become dominant, that is, athletes will severely lower their expectations for their performances (Goldfried, Decenteceo & Weinberg 1974). 'I never perform well against these athletes', 'I hate playing this team', 'I never do well in international competition', 'My performances are getting worse rather than improving', are examples of these negative orientations which can develop and subsequently detract from an athlete's potential performance. Usually with these situations it is wisest to seek speciaized psychological help to overcome the persistent problem. The coach does have one procedure which could be used but it involves a high degree of risk. Drastic changes in training programs, altered competition strategies, and/or new changes in competition preparations produce novelty effects which indicate that 'things will be different'. This gives rise to new hopes for the athlete. However, the risks of suddenly altering established procedures are great. They may be interpreted as 'panic', they may produce a scapegoat ('fire the Head Coach'), and/or they may not alleviate the real cause of the series of poor performances. If an alteration is engineered and it does not result in the anticipated performance improvement, then the situation is worsened further. The athlete's state becomes more problematical and the coach and/or organization lose credibility. Such drastic measures and gambles should only be made as a last resort and with a full realization of the risks involved. As far as altering generalized negative orientations which consitute the athlete's habitual thoughts, procedures might be instituted by an experienced, trained coach but they remain for discussion elsewhere as they are outside the scope of this book.

COACH OVER-REACTIONS

Often the coach inadvertently serves as a distraction from adequate competition preparations. At serious competitions coaches as well as athletes are stressed because of their emotional involvements with the athletes and the athletes' performances. Some coaches become agitated, others excited, and still others depressed and withdrawn. A common error at important competitions is for the coach to do something 'special'. This usually takes the form of giving lengthy, detailed and new sets of instructions to be followed in the competition just prior to the contest. This is something which is not normally done. An athlete's heightened arousal, coupled with a flood of information that cannot possibly be retained, and the interaction with the coach's 'strange' behaviours, serves to produce novel stresses with which most athletes cannot cope (Averill 1973). Many coaches fail at the time when they are needed to be their most adaptable and sensitive.

The best thing that a coach can do at serious competitions is to be consistent and attentive to the pre-planned preparatory procedures of athletes. Coaches should be aware of the complication effects that they could cause if they do not themselves remain under control and behave in a predictable, usual manner.

SOURCE OF INPUT

A further problem source is the lack of input from the athlete with regard to what should be done. A constant index of elite athletes is their desire to make decisions about their training and competition preparation in consultation with the coach (Rushall 1978b; Rushall & Garvie 1978; Rushall, Jamieson & Talbot 1977). If this is not done then there is an increased possibility that the coach will decide on incorrect or disagreeable competition content for the athlete. At least before very important competitions individual athlete meetings should be held to discuss and determine each athlete's competition preparation procedures. The wisdom of the athlete should be duly respected on such occasions.

Stress reaction properties of personal control depend upon the meaning of the control response for the athlete. What lends a competition preparation meaning is largely the context in which it is imbedded. This meaningfulness is heightened in a combined decision-making interaction between the coach and athlete. Behavioural, cognitive and decisional self-control is best when it is adaptive and practised, that is, relevant and meaningful (Averill 1973). Thus, even with coach-athlete counselling and discussion sessions the athlete will have to 'learn' how to interact in those situations.

SUMMARY

The above items are only some of those factors which cause performances to be hindered. As with any competent behaviour, an athlete needs to learn how to prepare and cope with the events that surround competitions. Thus, it is necessary to practise preparing for competitions and it is helpful to simulate as many stresses as possible so that coping procedures can be developed. The number of practices and simulations that are necessary varies with each athlete but that number is quite extensive. With some it may take a number of years. After each practice and/or simulation, there should be an evaluation of the experience which is aimed at improving the procedure that is being developed. Coping behaviours and feedback about their effectiveness together reduce stress. Coping without feedback is stress inducing (Averill 1973). The focus of these experiences should be on maintaining attention to the imminent sporting task while recognizing and coping with unexpected cues and events, thoughts of uncertainty, and distractions. An athlete's approach to competition should be characterized by consistent, predictable, task-specific behaviours and thoughts. To cope with each competition effectively, the athlete must recognize new events as quickly as possible and reorganize his/her behaviour in light of the new circumstances. Thus, an adaptive model which aims at maintaining maximal attention on the forthcoming performance but minimizes all unrelated and disruptive events is desirable.

3 General Procedures for Competition Preparation

The discussion in this chapter indicates some of the more important psychological ingredients which can be incorporated into the structure of competition preparations. The previous chapter indicated a number of sources from which stresses could arise for an athlete. The greater the number of stresses incurred by an individual, the greater will be the performance deterioration (Fenz 1974). It thus becomes a necessary coaching action that conditions be constructed for and skills developed in athletes whereby stresses will be minimized.

TEAM ORIENTATIONS

When a group of athletes is labelled a team, even though they may be a collection of individuals concerned with individual events, there are a number of benefits which can be derived. These benefits automatically acrue for actual teams. The handling of a 'team' becomes a necessary function of any sport.

Group discussion and the interactions and contributions of other athletes promote a greater degree of familiarization with the sport and its unique situations. This familiarization reduces conservative or hesitant attitudes that an athlete might have. Thus, athletes will become more experimenting, willing to try new things, and ready to attempt to progress at accelerated rates when exposed to group interaction processes. It is always a good practice to introduce new ideas and training or competition procedures in a group situation because each individual will be more receptive to the changes that are presented.

Individuals will be more adventurous, will seek a higher degree of risk, and/or will attempt to achieve higher levels of performance in team-oriented situations. The reason for this is said to be a diffusion of responsibility across the group. This feature can be enhanced when groups are organized that:

1. produce emotional bonds between members through group socials and public activities, and overt commitments to the group (cheers), and

2. free individuals from responsibilities for their performances once the performance is completed (that is, an absence of recriminations).

Team orientations also produce more adventurous actions in athletes because moderately risky behaviour has a stronger cultural value than caution. When individuals can appeal to an hypothesized entity such as 'the team' they are more capable of heroic performances than when self-oriented (Clark 1971).

Team concepts exert heightened influences on members who are at the extremes, that is, those who are very cautious or reserved and those who are very adventurous and extroverted. One should expect greater improvements in these individuals although improvements should be expected in all members.

There is one caution that must be heeded when promoting a sport group as a team. After an unexpectedly poor performance groups tend to lower their subsequent levels of aspiration more than they would as individuals. Thus, game and performance failures are better evaluated on an individual member basis rather than lambasting or admonishing the team. One of the desirable effects of this caution is that athlete morale is better maintained.

PUBLIC COMMITMENT

Performances of athletes are improved when there is a public statement made by the athlete of what the ensuing performance goal is (Botterill 1977; Wankel & McEwan 1976). This public commitment is more influential than privately determined goals (Levy 1977). Coaches need to develop pre-competition procedures whereby athletes indicate what their aims are. These are best proposed on the day of the competition.

Team coaches will need to devise individual goals for performance for each team member in consultation with each of them. For large teams, such as an American football team, this might be done in small groups. For example, the offensive line will not allow any quarterback 'sacks', the defensive line will limit the number of yards gained rushing, achieve a certain number of 'sacks', etc. For coaches of individual sports it is easier, as athletes need only indicate their proposed score, time, etc.

Producing public commitment does have its difficulties, particularly with individual events when there is more than one team member in the same event. This problem can be alleviated when each individual's event strategy is constructed. The committed performance should adhere to the principles which will be discussed in the section on goal setting. It should be remembered that it is the performance to be attained that is announced and not the goals that are specific for each individual and each competition.

REINTERPRETATION OF POTENTIALLY AVERSIVE
SITUATIONS

When an upcoming performance has the likelihood of producing poor competition results, that is, a defeat is very likely, the event can be reinterpreted so that the competition outcome can be masked or at least reduced in severity (Reid 1973). The most expedient method of doing this is to alter the performance goals. For example, in situations where winning is the only goal the major source of performance satisfaction stems from achieving that goal. But in circumstances where that goal is highly unlikely, if it still remains the goal then performance is likely to deteriorate dramatically.

What is more adaptive is to have the athletes still perform their best even though losing. It is better to have athletes performing not just for competition outcomes but to aim for self-improvement goals as well. This was a characteristic of elite athletes that was discussed in Chapter 1. In situations where winning is highly unlikely the goal emphases should be switched to ones which indicate self-improvement and provide a challenge for the performance. The scientific research involved with goal-setting indicates that performances are better when individuals strive for a number of goals in a single performance than when striving for a single goal (Atkinson & Reitman 1956).

The appropriate coaching strategy is therefore one of establishing a number of goals for all sporting performances. Those goals which have a high degree of negative potential for an effort should be minimized in their importance. Consequently, the goals which are stressed for each athlete will vary with each competitive situation and the likelihood of goal achievements.

INDIVIDUAL CONTROL

When an individual has control over a distractor or threat then he/she has a greater potential to display tolerance, persistence and consistency in performance (Averill 1973; House 1976). Thus, an athlete's confidence in his/her own abilities to achieve the goals which are established and the methods employed in the sporting task have a strong influence on the quality of performance (Kanfer & Seidner 1973).

The coaching response for producing a feeling of control in an athlete is to involve the athlete in goal-setting and the determination of pre-competition and competition behaviours, features which were evidenced in the characteristics of elite athletes.

CONTENT DECISION-MAKING

The decisions that are made to determine what is to be

done prior to and during competitions should be achieved by employing a number of criteria.

1. Plan to use behaviours which have been practised and proven to be successful.
2. Analyze the expected events and distractors by using objective criteria or verified observations.
3. Establish realistic goals (those which the athlete believes, not hopes, can be achieved).
4. Be very specific in the content of the plans, that is, indicate the exact behaviours to be followed rather than using vague and ambiguous terms such as 'loosen-up', 'hustle', 'stick-it-to-them', etc.

Specific behavioural plans can reduce the amount of uncertainty and interpretive distraction that can result from vague, unrehearsed instructions. The plans also should include a realistic interpretation of the sensations which will be experienced including pain and fatigue. The anticipation of sensations, even though they are aversive, reduces the degree of threat and anxiety which could result in the situation (Averill 1973). Probable negative situations are reduced in their stressfulness if preparations precede their occurence. The preparations are very effective if the characteristics of the experience and how to behave in the situation are fore-warned and planned (Coles, Herzberger, Sperber & Goetz 1975). Detailed behavioural plans are called *strategies*. When several performances involve modifications of a general theme (e.g. the athlete's strengths), the variability between them is reduced (Vestewig 1978). The consistent structuring of performance strategies facilitates performance consistency to the point where the athlete's performances become more predictable (Magnusson & Ekehammar 1978). Strategy development and practice reduce problems and increase behavioural coping capacity in the competitive situation (Hollandsworth, Glazeski & Dressel 1978).

It becomes necessary for coaches to develop detailed game and performance strategies in conjunction with athletes.

The behaviours of better athletes prior to and during competitions are characterized by:

1. an ability to adjust up or down when task demands change (a capacity to cope),
2. a high degree of preparedness and performance readiness control between performances and during delays, and
3. an equal emphasis on performance preparation and performance (Vanek & Cratty 1970).

AROUSAL

The relationship between arousal and physical performance has been a much researched topic. The conclusions of all the studies really have not produced a definitive statement as to how the level of excitedness or arousal of an individual affects athletic performance. Even recently, attempts have been made to reconcile the indecisions which still exist (Singer 1977). One interpretation that can be offered for this lack of a precise statement is that the relationship is not universal and applicable to all persons but rather, that there are differing relationships depending upon the groups of people considered. There have been many presentations which have been offered about arousal and performance and this section contains this writer's analysis of the relationship between arousal and athletic performance and its relevance for the practitioner.

What is Known About Arousal

There are several principles involving arousal and performance about which there is little debate.

1. The more aroused is an individual then the more restricted is the range of information and cues that can be utilized (Easterbrook 1959). This means that performances that are dependent upon making fine discriminations (e.g. rifle-shooting, archery, chess) require relatively low levels of arousal. Sport performances which

are not dependent on processing much information (e.g. power-lifting, football linemen, shot-putting) require quite high levels of arousal. When considering this principle, the reader must remember that these levels are relative for each athlete. The consideration of each individual's relative arousal level between various tasks is paramount when preparing for serious competitions.

2. Elite athletes have higher levels of arousal for an optimum level of performance than do lesser abilitied athletes (Barry 1979; Genov 1970b; Ryan 1970). A characteristic of superior athletes is that they 'crank-up' more for a performance than do others.

Two factors for assessing whether an athlete is at the level of arousal that will facilitate a good performance then are the task demands (the more complex the activity, the less the arousal), and the experience-performance level of the athlete.

Two Theories

There are two general theories which postulate a relationship between arousal and athletic performance. These will be discussed briefly.

The inverted-U hypothesis. This is illustrated in Figure 1 and it indicates that *for a specific task* there is an optimum level of arousal which produces a maximum performance given that all cognitive factors (thoughts) remain constant. Thus, it is possible to be aroused either too much or too little to the detriment of the performance. There is much evidence to support this theory but just as much to refute it. In the field of athletics it is a phenomenon that has been observed mainly in lesser abilitied athletes (Barry 1979; Fiorini 1978). What complicates this assertion is that if the thoughts which accompany a task performance change then the nature of the task is changed and the optimal level of arousal shifts. This is important for coaching elite performers. If the thought processes prior to performance can

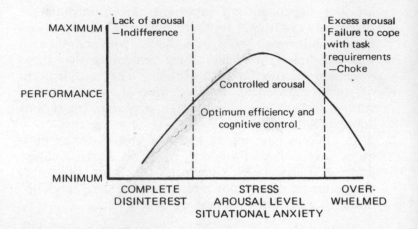

Figure 1. A stylized presentation of the relationship of arousal to performance as proposed by adherents of the inverted-U hypothesis.

be consistent then an optimal level of performance arousal can be developed. But, coaches and athletes should be aware that if athletes let their pre-competition patterns of behaviour and thinking vary greatly between performances, then their performances will be similarly inconsistent. The athlete is faced with the task of matching a new optimum level of arousal with a new set of behaviours and stimuli each time he/she performs. Hence, the probability of matching an optimal arousal level with the varying performance preparation circumstances is very low. The implication of this for coaching is clear: systematize the pre-competition behaviours and thoughts of athletes. A cautionary note should be made with this recommendation. The stylization of pre-competition behaviours should only be started after a certain amount of experience in competition. Just what that 'certain amount' is is not known at this time. Coaches, at present, are the best persons to determine when the development process should be started.

The drive hypothesis. This theory is exampled by Figure 2. It proposes that the higher the level of arousal then the better

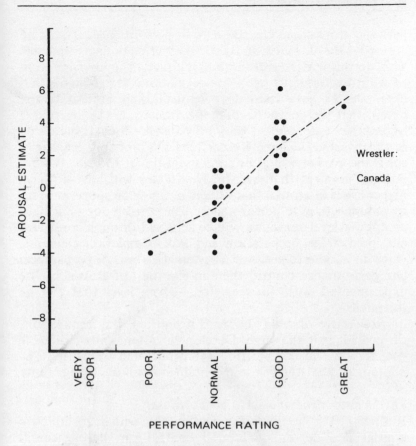

Figure 2. The relationship of arousal to standards of performance for an elite Canadian wrestler. The linearity of the trend is quite noticeable and demonstrates the assertions of a drive hypothesis.

the performance. Two recent studies, one with basketball players (Fiorini 1978) and the other with wrestlers (Barry 1979) have presented evidence to support this theory as being applicable to elite athletes. In those same studies lesser athletes exhibited a number of relationships some of which were of an inverted-U pattern. What is consistent is that with elite athletes there is a positive, linear relationship between arousal and the standard of performance. The more aroused is the elite athlete, the better will be the performance. This, to this writer's satisfaction, is a fact. The interpretation of why this occurs is open to speculation. It is possible that elite athletes have learned to control their arousal to the extent that they never become too aroused, in the inverted-U hypothesis sense, and so they only display the left-hand side of the inverted-U curve. Researchers will probably eventually solve the reason why. For the practitioner though, the important point is that eventually athletes will have to have higher levels of arousal than others in the same sport, in order to produce an elite performance. The consistency to achieve an optimal level of arousal will be achieved through consistent and predictable preparation and task completion elements. Once an athlete establishes a systematic form of preparation and performance control then an elevation of arousal can be experimented with to seek the highest level that can be tolerated.

Irrespective of what theory is supported, the implications for coaching are the same. Develop consistent and predictable preparation and competition behaviours and thoughts. The content of these items should contain arousal provoking events.

The Measurement of an Athlete's Arousal

Rushall (1975) presented a method by which an athlete's arousal and degree of arousal control can be measured. This tool is presented in Appendix B. It contains 23 descriptive symptoms of arousal, an arousal level scale (Dermer & Berscheid 1972), and an estimate of winning scale. This checklist was used by Barry (1979), Fiorini (1978), and Rushall (1977a) to assess features of arousal in athletes just prior to performance. What has been revealed through using this pre-competition checklist in research studies is a series of facts about elite athlete competition preparations.

1. Varying levels of arousal are related to various patterns of arousal symptons. When an athlete is moderately

aroused one set of symptoms is consistently experienced. When an athlete is highly aroused a different set of symptoms is consistently experienced and reported. It is apparent that elite athletes can differentiate themselves when they are and are not highly aroused as well as the differing sensations which accompany the various arousal levels. This capacity is not evidenced in inexperienced or lower calibre athletes.

2. The higher the level of arousal and therefore the existence of a particular pattern of symptoms, the better the level of performance. It is possible to predict the level of performance that will be emitted by recognizing the pattern of arousal symptoms which are indicated prior to a performance. This raises the possibility of devising pre-competition actions that will produce the pattern of symptoms which precede the highest level of performance. This strategem was reported by Rushall (1977a) in an international wrestling meet.

The use of the pre-competition checklist aids the coach and athlete to determine the following factors.

1. The existence of controlled arousal which is evidenced when distinct behaviour symptom patterns of arousal are consistently demonstrated for locatable levels of performance.

2. The adequacy of arousal levels is revealed when a linear relationship is evidenced between immediate pre-competition arousal levels and performance standards.

3. The definition of the most desirable symptoms which should exist prior to a competition.

Implications of Arousal for Competition Preparation

Several features concerning arousal warrant consideration for developing pre-competition and competition procedures.

The focus of attention should be limited to task-relevant

factors. If athletes also focus on distractions and self-oriented factors then they will need a lower level of arousal because of the increased number of cues which need attention. The lower level of arousal will reduce the potential quality and amplitude of the performance output. Thus, by narrowing the focus of attention as much as possible, that is, limiting the number of cues which must be attended to, higher levels of arousal can be developed to increase the standard of performance output.

Control of arousal is developed by the coach and athlete working together using the feedback generated by a measuring device such as that which is included in the appendices of this text. The development process is not rapid. It takes a long time and in reality is never achieved to the point that a total consistency can be attained by an athlete. The inconsistency is caused by the varying nature and unique aspects of every competition situation. The process is designed to minimize the inconsistency.

Deliberate arousal developing behaviours and procedures should be planned and experimented with to the point of familiarity that a predictable level of high arousal can be achieved. These should be included in the pre-competition plans.

SUMMARY

As a means of summarizing this chapter the work of Filip Genov (1970a) will be reviewed. Competition preparation is viewed as being comprized of two components, 'general readiness' which results from physical activity and is analagous to physiological arousal, and 'concrete mobilization readiness' which is analagous to specific, task-oriented thought activity. The terms for the two concepts may differ but they are very similar. Genov listed 12 influential factors for the development of an appropriate psychological-physical readiness for performance.

1. The structure and content of performance preparation is dependent upon the type of activity. Thus, even

within the same sport but for differing events, the preparations will be different.

2. Performance preparation is more effective the higher the level of performance classification of the athlete. Hence, pre-competition preparations become more and more important as the skill level of the athlete increases.

3. The surroundings and conditions of the competition affect performance readiness. Unfamiliar situations and events reduce the degree of readiness (unless adequate coping strategies exist).

4. The personal and social importance for attaining the performance goals affect the amount or level of readiness. The incentives (goals) for performance affect the measure of preparation that is required.

5. The athlete's self-assessment of the preparation and determination to achieve goals affects the readiness to perform. Self-developed and self-controlled preparations maximize this feature.

6. The greater the degree of difficulty of the contest then the higher the level of readiness that is required. The more serious the competition then the more intense the preparations and the higher the level of arousal will have to be.

7. The experience of the athlete in forming similar states of readiness affects the degree of effect of the preparation. Thus, preparations are skills which need to be learned and practised.

8. Reduced health states, fatigue, or injury require greater conscious efforts to prepare adequately for a performance.

9. The emotional state prior to the commencement of preparations affects the application to and standard of readiness. Thus, it is necessary to eradicate unfavourable circumstances and to develop a good positive atmosphere and attitude in the athlete before pre-competition activities.

10. Competition readiness is hindered if insufficient time is

available. The more difficult the contest, then the greater is the time required to achieve peak preparedness.

11. Competition preparations are peculiar to the athlete. The activities must be personalized for each individual.

12. The skill ability in mental rehearsal of the athlete and the physical content of the preparations affects the level of readiness that is achieved. Thus, the content of preparations needs to be experimented with, evaluated, and altered where necessary.

The above characteristics govern the level of preparedness of the athlete. The preparedness is greatly affected by the athlete's appraisal of the competition circumstance and its social and personal importance. This appraisal can be altered through adopting a team orientation towards the competition, the use of public commitment, the stressing of the importance of various goals imbedded in multiple-goal incentives, the maximizing of the athlete's control over preparations, and the structured content of the performance strategy according to sound psychological principles.

4 Important Characteristics of Competition Strategies

There are two major strategies which need to be developed as a preparation procedure for serious competition. The first strategy contains all the behaviours which need and might need to be done prior to the commencement of the competitive performance. The second strategy comprizes all the physical and mental behaviours which need to be performed in the competitive effort. The performance strategy contains all the preferred behaviours (the primary performance strategy) which are emitted as long as they are adequate for the performance. There is at least one alternate coping behaviour for each of the preferred behaviours which is used should the primary performance behaviour prove to be inadequate for the circumstances which arise during the competition. The central feature of any strategy is one of coping with unexpected circumstances and events so that an athlete's attentional control and progress is maintained toward goal achievement.

THE COPING SKILL

Coping strategies are better than strategies which have no coping alternatives for producing performance output and tolerance to stress (Andrew 1968; Meichenbaum & Turk 1975). Predicting and preparing for problems will produce better tolerance and coping responses in performance (Aderman, Bryant & Domelsmith 1978).

The ability to cope with all the possible distractors which may occur in a sporting contest is never fully realized.

Through a constant learning and adaptive process, athletes should develop knowledge of and should have experienced the behaviours required to handle the various stressors and distractors which occur in a sport and in particular its competitive situations. The degree of acquaintance with these behaviours determines the stage of transition for an athlete from being an inexperienced athlete to becoming an experienced athlete. All sources of input (e.g. coach, other athletes, officials, team support personnel, etc.) which can shed light on the circumstances surrounding competition should be used when developing strategies.

The procedure for developing a coping strategy is two-stage. First, the pre-competition and competition situations are analyzed and planned in minute detail. Usually, the pre-competition factors will be more numerous and varied than the competition factors. Pre-competition factors include sleeping arrangements and facilities; meal times, availability, and variety; uniform readiness; transportation availability and the time to the facility; competition times; warm-up facilities and schedules; competition facilities; officiating procedures and briefings; audience characteristics; emergency services; announcing procedures; personal habits and preferences; warm-up activities; mental preparation requirements; etc. The list of these factors is very long and will contain a number of items which are peculiar to each competition venue, organization and sport. The competition factors will depend upon the sport being played and the strategy for the athlete's conduct in the contest. For each aspect of the competition day's activities the following features should be determined; what will happen, what could result from the occurrence of each particular event; how will the events affect each athlete, and what actions are appropriate for all events. For each of the situations that are deemed to be important, whether it be pre-competition or competition, both a primary and a coping behaviour strategy should be developed. The strategies should be constructed in the expression style (the way the athlete talks to him/herself) of the athlete so that it contains the utmost meaning for the individual (Maier 1972). It should stress the behaviours to be done, the content decision should be primarily the athlete's (Kanfer & Seidner 1973), and it should incorporate positive task-oriented content (Barber & Hahn 1962). After the initial strategy is developed it should be evaluated and modified where necessary after each use so that it is constantly refined (Averill 1973). Each competitive situation will require some modifications that are unique to that circumstance. Competition planning is a required activity for all serious competitions. It can no longer be neglected or treated in the haphazard fashion that is commonly practised by both coaches and athletes.

The second stage for developing a coping capacity is to practise the strategies. The ability of an athlete to cope with sporting situations is a developed skill. Coaches can do much to accelerate the learning process to produce this capacity. A planned, gradual introduction of the competition behaviours, performance goals and simulations, and distractors should be instituted with the athletes having a high degree of probability for success with each successive stage of the exposure (Orne 1965). This means that once an athlete is successful at coping with one degree of situational difficulty it should then be increased in its complexity and difficulty. The progressive positive experiences of coping have desirable attitudinal and behavioural outcomes when contrasted to the more common total immersion circumstances of stress introduction, that is, athletes are exposed to serious competitions for the first time with little preparation or schooling (Wolff, Krasnegor & Farr 1965). The implication of this fact is that coaches have to plan the development of psychological coping behaviours in great detail and for their implementation to cover an extended period of time. They should occupy as much emphasis in the training program as physical development and skill training. They certainly warrant the time and energy that is required to develop them.

Coping behaviours are determined by prior experiences. There are three forms of experience that can be used to yield practices for producing coping repertoires.

The first form is real experience gained through competing in varied situations. The outcomes of these circumstances can have positive and negative effects. Close monitoring of the athlete, the provision of support services, and a detailed de-briefing session aimed at determining what can be learned from each experience are desirable organizational features surrounding real competitions. It is a popular opinion that real experience is the most desirable form of experience. However, the opportunities for learning experiences to be gained from competition are rarely used to their maximum. There is a potential for the beneficial effects of competition to be elevated if sound preparatory steps and post-performance evaluations are employed.

The second form of experience is through contrived events. This usually takes the form of simulation of competition events and conditions, the practice of pre-competition behaviours such as altering rest, exercise and eating times to counteract jet-lag, doing warm-ups, trying-out competition equipment, and the over-stress of potential distractors. This can even be carried into the final stages of preparation. Elite athletes indicated that the content of their warm-up activities were simulations or practices of what would be done in competition. The outcomes of these experiences should be positive. If they are not, then they should be repeated with the necessary modifications until they are successfully completed.

The third form of experience is imaginary. This entails the mental rehearsal of various situations and events and the execution of the successful primary and coping behaviours associated with them. These experiences should always be positive. They can be performed at the athlete's own discretion but the frequency of performance should be monitored by the coach. Elite athletes indicated that they used mental rehearsal as much as possible prior to competition. It is also helpful to perform mental rehearsal after a successful contrived or real experience. That guarantees that the imagery is successful and correct in detail and serves to reinforce the learning potential of the experience. The mental rehearsal of coping behaviours is enhanced in its effect if it is performed while the athlete is in a totally relaxed state (see the chapter on relaxation).

PROLONGED EVENTS

For events which span a long period of time, for example, hockey, football, marathon runs, distance swims, etc., it is best to develop strategies which cover segments of the activity. Thus, the term 'segmenting a strategy' is often used. In these circumstances the competition is broken into a series of mini-strategies with each segment containing its own goals, content, description of sensations and coping responses. Each segment is dependent upon the outcomes of the segment which precedes it. Thus, if the first possession of the ball in American football results in a major score, the next segment will be affected differently than were the outcome of the first possession a failure to make a first down.

Elite athletes suggested a segmenting approach to competition by their admission of seeking to establish an early contest lead irrespective of the cost. Segmenting works, because as the delay interval for the attainment of a goal increases, as is the case when only a terminal goal is set, the subjective value of that goal decreases. Long-term goals are not very influential although they can be easily verbalized (House 1973).

Although this segmenting appears to be obvious it is rarely planned. One feature which must be considered is that the psychological climate during a competition can change very suddenly. Such a change affects the behaviours of athletes. Part of a competition strategy needs to take this possibility into account. Segmented game strategies allow for adjustments in the game-plan to be instituted if necessary on some pre-planned basis. The recognition of the occurrence of change effects, the need for segmented alternative strategies, and the stage-wise appraisal of performance is now being displayed in professional sports, particularly American football.

Extended duration events require athletes to concentrate on parts of a total strategy in sequence. The size of each segment is determined by the athlete's capacity and the nature of the sport.

A goal should be established for each segment in the strategy series (Botterill 1977). The performance and behaviours of each segment should have an immediate goal objective. The goal is current and relevant to immediate events. This increases the degree of task-relevant thinking since performance outcomes will be contingent upon behavioural adequacy. This contrasts markedly with the more usual attempt to achieve remote aims. In that situation, the consequences of early segment behaviours are not nearly as obvious or influential upon an athlete's behaviours. When the final outcome of the total competition is the sole determinant of performance adequacy, there is a reduction in an athlete's response flexibility and the ability to adjust to situational factors. These two features are enhanced by intermediate segment goals which indicate progress towards the final goals.

Thus, a competitive strategy that has been segmented requires the athlete to enter the contest and concentrate on achieving an immediate goal, that is, the goal of the first segment. When that is achieved, the next segment goal is the aim of the performance. This means that the athlete does not think of the ultimate goal but rather the goal of each section. This is a very important departure from the normal approach to competition of trying to achieve a relatively remote end result. An added advantage to segmenting is that if the segment goal is not achieved coping and recovery procedures can be implemented deliberately and with control in the next segment. This avoids the onset of panic and/or imminent failure.

GOAL-SETTING

There are extensive researches which have investigated the effects of setting goals on performance. The findings that have been published have direct implications for the coaching of athletes. Dimitrova (1970) summarized the major principles.

1. The setting of goals increases work output as much as 50% over that achieved when no goals are set. The content of training programs should always include goals to be achieved. For training items where goals (performance criteria) are not established, athletes will produce efforts which do not facilitate maximal adaptation. Thus, better athlete training efforts will be achieved when performance goals and evaluations are provided for each training item. A similar effect occurs for competition. Elite athletes respond to self-determined, publicly committed goals.

2. The goals that are set for training and competition should have a high probability of achievement. When failure is imminent performance deteriorates. Thus, the goals which are emphasized within the multi-incentive package for a performance must be within the athlete's achievement capability.

3. The standard and volume of work achieved is higher when goals are publicly expressed (public commitment).

4. The frequent indication of performance adequacy leads to a higher probability of achievement of final remote goals. As was indicated above, frequent indications of performance progress (the attainment of intermediate goals) maintains positive, motivated efforts in prolonged events.

5. The more clear and detailed the goal, the greater is the tolerance of fatigue and distractions. This is enhanced when an athlete knows what to achieve and how to achieve it through the use of a detailed, planned competition strategy.

6. In the majority of athletic events where fatigue or aversive circumstances are experienced, there is a stage where an athlete questions continuing at a constant level of effort. Dimitrova calls this a 'stopping wish'. This is usually after about 80-85% of the activity has been completed independent of the work goal. At that stage the probability of attaining the goal should be high, that is, the athlete is on schedule for attaining the final goal, and the procedures for continuing are clearly formulated, as detailed in a performance strategy.

MULTIPLE GOALS

Although a performance outcome may be singular, that is, the height jumped, the time driven, the number of tackles achieved, the interpretation of the results of a performance can be many and varied. Performances are enhanced when the final evaluation indicates the possible attainment of a number of positive outcomes (Atkinson & Reitman 1956). Thus, the rowing of a race and the performance produced could be evaluated in terms of

1. winning or placing,
2. an improvement in time,
3. the correct execution of some technical aspect which may be different for each crew member,
4. the generation of information (what was learned from the race) which may be different for each crew member,
5. the relationship of the performance to another crew's performances, and
6. the contribution of points to a team effort.

Naturally, there are other interpretations that could be added to the above list. The indication to the athletes involved in the above exampled race is that there are a variety of outcomes to be achieved through the single performance. If the absolute goal of winning is not attained then there are still many benefits and positive outcomes that are possible. The inventiveness of the coach will determine the types of multiple goals which are set for performance. It is essential that some self-evaluation of individual goals be established for each contest within the list of goals.

Multiple goals are especially important for teams. Team performance goals, both intermediate and final, can be augmented with performance goals, both intermediate and final, for each player (Forward & Zander 1971). If the outcome of the team's effort is positive, a re-setting of those goals is possible for the next performance. If the team goals are not achieved, then individual player analyses should be undertaken rather than admonishing the team as was explained earlier.

DETERMINING GOALS

If goals are to be established, who should set them? If athletes alone establish goals there is every likelihood that they will vary and gradually become easier (Flexibrod & O'Leary 1973). Elite athletes wish to be involved in the determination of the performance goals in consultation with the coach (Rushall & Garvie 1978; Rushall, Jamieson & Talbot 1977). The role of the coach in this situation is one of producing the impression in the athlete that he/she is responsible for the major input into the goal decision-making. The coach monitors the scope of the goal so that it is constant in its direction for improvement and it is of sufficient difficulty to be very challenging without being unrealistic.

The degree of difficulty for goals is a very individual decision. With elite athletes the standards for performance should be gradually raised even when a previous standard has not been achieved (Lupfer & Jones 1971). Generally, the higher the expectation for a performance, the higher the standard of performance whether or not the goal is achieved (Dimitrova 1970; Locke 1966; Locke & Bryan 1966). To use this principle the coach has to orchestrate a mix of successes and failures in goal attainment so as not to decrease the athlete's motivation through continued failure. An athlete or coach should never be complacent with a performance or ever consider that an ultimate performance level has been achieved. The de-briefing analysis of the level of attainment of each of the multiple-goals and the execution of both the pre-competition and competition strategies usually indicates features which can be improved upon for the next performance, that is, a deficiency did occur in the performance. Detailed feedback is a necessary characteristic in order that goal-setting may affect performance (Erez 1977). Both positive and negative aspects of a performance should be stressed, each in their rightful proportion. In terms of setting goal difficulty for elite athletes it would be better to err on the side of being too difficult than being too lenient.

SOME CRITERIA FOR ESTABLISHING GOALS

The following items are a number of criteria that should always be considered when establishing goals for sporting competitions.

1. They should be measurable. Objective evaluation criteria and performance limits should be stated where possible.
2. They should be accepted by all those involved (the athlete, coach, team, parents, administrators, etc.). Thus, they are pre-planned and determined in some social context.
3. Goals should be related to performance. This allows them to act as performance guidelines and for performance evaluations.
4. When there is more than one goal, as with multiple-goals, there should be priorities and guidelines established for resolving goal conflicts which, hopefully, will not occur.
5. Goals should be realistic but challenging. They should be adjusted up or down should frustration or complacency be exhibited.
6. Goals should be related to other parts of the organization (overall club aims, national status, etc.).

7. Goals are structured primarily to improve and, in some cases, maintain performance levels and characteristics.

SUMMARY

There are two strategies which need to be developed for competition; those behaviours to be performed prior to the contest and those which are required in the contest. For each preferred strategy item there should be at least one alternative behaviour should the preparations and contest not proceed as planned. This is the coping process that lessens the effect of disruptions, distractions and unplanned performance trends and outcomes. The practice of strategies lessens the threat of contest and stressful situations. Practice can be real, contrived or imaginary, each having its own uses and benefits. For some sports the competitions are too long to be treated as a single event. It is advantageous to break the contest into meaningful segments, each with its own behaviours, immediate goals and coping reactions. The goals for both segments and the total performance should be multiple and established by the coach and the athlete together.

5   Suggested Content for Pre-competition Strategies

Pre-competition strategies encompass all those activities which precede competition on the day of the contest. For some athletes this period of time may have to be extended to a number of days. This chapter discusses some of the important characteristics of the pre-competition strategy.

WAKE-UP PROCEDURES

How a person feels when he/she first wakes in the morning very often influences that person's attitudes and behaviours for the day. Those who are able to develop 'happy thoughts' tolerate and handle frustrations, problems and distractions better than those persons who have negative dispositions (Mischel, Ebbesen & Zeiss 1973). It is possible to learn to execute a brief, effective procedure that will generate a positive attitude immediately upon waking at the start of the day. This is necessary so that the athlete's reactions and adaptations for the rest of the day will be more effective than if it were not controlled and a negative initial attitude were developed. This could have a detrimental effect on the rest of the day's happenings and events.

Some suggested steps for developing a waking procedure are listed below.

1. Wake slowly.
2. Rehearse a number of positive self-statements until fully awake. For example, 'I feel good', 'I am ready to

go', 'This is going to be a great day', 'That stretch makes my legs feel so good', etc.

3. Slowly stretch the whole body in a routine similar to that described in the chapter on relaxation. One would not do the actual relaxation routine because of the possibility of going to sleep again. The stretching and positive self-statements can be done concurrently.

4. Smile deliberately and maintain it until the wake-up procedure is completed.

5. Continue the above routine until a 'good' feeling is recognized.

When to terminate the waking routine is left to the discretion of the athlete. It should not be hurried and it will vary in the length of time required each day. It would be best to err on the side of spending too much time on this action than too little.

The state of a person's receptivity is heightened during these initial waking moments because the amount and complexity of stimuli being received is quite low. Consequently, any positive self-talk that is engaged in and any emphasis on feeling good through controlled stretching is very effective because they are emphasized with respect to the lack of other stimulation. They produce a state which serves as a comparative basis for evaluating and coping with the events which are encountered for the rest of the day. Wake-up procedures should also be used as a way of terminating rest periods.

Practice at waking in this manner is required to develop an effective skill in using it. Coach monitoring of the process development and an emphasis on the importance of it will motivate athletes to persevere with the learning practices. It has been found useful for athletes to place some sign or reminder next to their beds in a very prominent position to remind them to rehearse the wake-up routine upon rising during the learning stage. After several trials, the routine and its behaviours will be emitted as a learned segment of the initial chain of behaviours which follow sleep or rest.

GENERAL ACTIVITY PLANNING

An assumption is made here that athletes will be specially housed prior to serious competition. Athletes will not be living at home. This action allows the coach and athlete to have more control over their activities and it removes one major source of emotional stress (home-life). What is considered here is that a number of athletes are housed in the same locale such as a motel or hotel.

The day's events prior to getting ready for the contest should be planned to include essential activities. Other distractions or happenings can be tolerated around the scheduling of events such as:

1. what and when to eat,
2. when to visit the physiotherapist, get taped, shave, etc.,
3. when to and what form of rest or mild activity is required,
4. equipment check,
5. when to travel to the contest site,
6. when to rehearse the event mentally,
7. when to check for anxiety levels and confidence levels, and
8. when to warm-up.

A feature in this planning would be that the events are normal for the athlete, that is, they have been practised and he/she is accustomed to them. The athlete should be familiar and satisfied with the routine even though it may seem strange and regimented to the uninitiated outside observer. It would be erroneous to expect an athlete to perform and tolerate a strategy of self-control behaviours without having experienced them before a serious competition. The reason behind this is that a stressful competition could heighten the effect of the new routine to be so contrasted to what is 'normal' for the athlete that the advantages to be derived from the structured procedure may be far outweighed by the extra stress caused through lack of familiarity (Epuran, Horghidan & Muresanu 1970).

Most elite or advanced athletes have some behaviours

which are performed with reasonable consistency on the day
of competition.   The planning of a normal routine would
mainly concern systematizing the procedures, adding some
beneficial activities or restrictions in behaviour, plus planning
for coping with distractions or problems.

Rest

Rest periods are helpful as methods for maintaining an
acceptable range of arousal level or guarding against fatigue.
If a competition occurs at night it would not be advisable to
allow extended tours, shopping sprees, visitations to or with
relatives, etc., during the day.   Rest periods serve to periodically narrow the span of attention of the athlete to an
environment that is related to the imminent task. A bout of
relaxation may be employed to produce and control the
desirable effects of the rest period (Kovatchev 1973).

Group Activities

Group interactions and activities should be allowed and
mildly encouraged when athletes are housed together. This is
because stress reactions are reduced in groups.   It may be
necessary to manipulate group memberships if there is a
possibility of potential personality conflicts or if members
are to compete against each other in forthcoming events.
If the coach circulates among the groups which form, it may
be advantageous for him/her to initiate discussions about
forthcoming competition plans and expectations with each
group.   This serves as a ploy for not allowing the focus of
attention of the athletes to vary to any appreciable extent.

Loss of Confidence

What can be done if an athlete loses confidence, that is,
negative thoughts about him/herself and the impending
performance occur? The only approach at this time of preparation is to effect a variety of positive self-talk or imagery
procedures (Meichenbaum 1975; Schwartz & Gottman 1974).
The following activities could be used:

1. relaxation with positive imagery of self and environmental coping;
2. mental rehearsal of the forthcoming activity, and
3. simulation of part of the activity, such as skill practices with evaluation, performing part of a race at race pace, running through some plays, etc.

These activities should be repeated until the athlete regains confidence. Careful, seemingly objective justification for the athlete being able to perform to expectation by the coach can also provide cues for the athlete to re-interpret his/her negative appraisal to a positive appraisal.

Increase in Tension

If an athlete becomes too aroused too early then he/she should participate in distraction activities which allow sufficient physical activity to dissipate unnecessary tensions. Diversion activities such as playing cards, Monopoly, Scrabble (the group situation dissipates the tension in these activities), shuffle board, table tennis, pool and walking provide sufficient distraction and tension outlet to relieve problems. Reading, writing letters and watching TV may be too passive to be effective relief activities for exaggerated tension. One can also allow longer warm-ups with less effort or even allow an extra workout with little quality work to serve as very specific distractors with physical outlet activities. It should be pointed out that these extra sessions of sport specific work have the added advantage of maintaining the attention focus of the athlete within a relatively narrow range.

The problem that occurs with the pre-competition period is that the athlete has to bide his/her time until the very structured section of the preparation for performance begins. During this period there is little that can be done to enhance performance. There is every opportunity for events to happen which will detract from the performance. Thus, the objective within this time period is to minimize the chances of performance-debilitating events happening.

The athlete has occasionally to monitor his/her own level

of arousal, confidence and type of activity. The times for periodically checking these states are planned in the pre-competition strategy and if the self-assessment indicates an unfavourable state the necessary corrective routines should be automatically performed. Elite athletes indicated the ability to recover from these states so it is important for the coach to develop instructional sessions and content to teach athletes how to perform these coping procedures.

AT THE SITE OF COMPETITION
The activities which are participated in at the competition site should constitute competition preparation and be totally planned. Even if some time is spent spectating on-going activities, the amount of time doing that is planned. The preparation for the competitive performance should be planned, practised and predictable for both primary and coping strategies.

Relaxation
Some athletes initiate their preparations with a session of relaxation and positive imagery. This practice is quite common in Eastern European countries. It has the advantage of producing an identifiable level of arousal from which to start the competition preparation procedures. It masks the effects of previous events which may have caused excessive or uncontrolled arousal and anxiety (Kazdin 1974). In essence, it is a form of self-calibration (see Figure 3).

Warm-up
The activities in the warm-up are selected to produce a number of effects. The central termperature of the muscles can be increased, the range of movement of the joints can be increased to an adequate amount, the neuromuscular patterns to be used in the activity can be facilitated, and the attention of the athlete can be narrowed. The athlete decides what activities are to be performed in the warm-up.

In making decisions about warming-up the athlete should

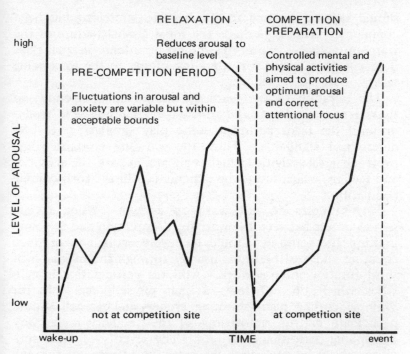

Figure 3. An example of the control of arousal prior to competition. Prior to the actual competition preparation activities, considerable variations in arousal are tolerated. A bout of relaxation reduces the amount of arousal to a baseline level. This is used as the starting point and initial procedure for the competition preparations at the contest site. From then on, mental and physical activities which have been planned and practised produce a controlled elevation of arousal to the optimal level.

be able to justify the purpose behind each activity unit. The coach should expect most athletes to do most of their warm-up activities by themselves as is done by elite athletes. With team games it is necessary to stipulate when team activities will start so that individual activities can be planned around them. The nature of some of the warm-up content should be of the same quality and intensity as that which will occur in competition which is also a feature of elite athlete preparations. These bouts of pace work or play simulations should not be invoked until adequate stretching has been completed. This is perhaps the most crucial feature of the warm-up activity. Warm-ups should be intense in quality as it is a further means for attending totally to the impending task.

The duration of the warm-up should be open-ended so that it is continued until the athlete feels that he/she is 'ready' or until the team performs some play simulations to pre-determined standards. Thus, the warm-up contains some overt rehearsal activities which replicate, in part, the activities and feelings which are to be experienced in the forthcoming competition.

Most athletes do not warm-up enough. When a time period occurs between the warm-up completion and the competition the warm-up should be severe enough to produce sweating and breathlessness usually through the inclusion of short-duration intense work. Athletes participating in activities which do not have a high physiological toll, for example, curling, pistol shooting, archery and baseball, should participate in true simulations of their activity under very demanding performance criteria. The severity of these activities should be such that the warm-up effects last through the time period to the contest. This is particularly important for the effects on skilled activities.

Pre-competition Behaviours

Between the completion of a warm-up and the entrance into competition is a crucial period. At this time athletes are susceptible to the influence of minor events which can be magnified in their importance. The activities during this period should maintain the warmth and range of movement attained in the warm-up. Athletes should keep active and warm and continue periodic bouts of stretching if the physiological effects of warm-up are important. The primary concern during this time is to focus on task relevant factors and to deny any distractors. This feature is required for both individual and team sport preparations.

Some features to be planned at this stage of preparation are listed below.

1. Determine when to report to the coach. Hopefully, the coach will not require the athlete to attend to new information. This consultation should be an opportunity to evaluate if any last minute adjustments need to be made. A brief recitation of a part of a mental rehearsal of the competition strategy is a good method of monitoring the athlete's focus of attention. A review of the initial part or segment of a team-game strategy is helpful. It produces little effect to attempt to cover the whole game strategy as the goals suggested will be too remote and the information too voluminous if done in detail or too vague if done in general terms.

2. As the time for the competitive effort approaches, the amount of physical activity performed by the athlete should increase. This is necessary to aid in the development of high arousal levels. Increased stretching, walking with more violent activities being used, will help elevate the level.

3. Athletes should be isolated from other competitors, well-meaning visitors, and the opportunity to view other competitions. This is a feature which should be considered for inclusion in team sports. When athletes are not competing, or waiting for a shift or a substitution during a game, they should be participating in activities which will increase their concentration on task-relevant factors. The commonly observed spectator activities (watching others perform) which occur at this time serve as distractors and possibly are more detrimental than helpful to performance because of changing the athlete's focus of attention.

4. Mental rehearsals should be practised as is done by elite athletes. These serve to maintain concentration on task-relevant rather than self-oriented thoughts. The positive content aspects of mental rehearsal also help to produce

an approach orientation to the competitive effort.

5. Emit some positive self-statements (Meichenbaum 1975; Schwartz & Gottman 1974). Talking to oneself is helpful. 'I am able to perform my best', 'You will set the tempo for the match', 'They had better watch out as we are ready' are samples of positive self-statements. There is some suggestion that using the second person for expression even makes them more effective. This form of expression should be compared to negative statements which express hope and doubt, for example, 'I hope that I can do my best', 'If I can just score some points'. While the athlete is active in this period it may be helpful to concentrate on the content of the positive self-imagery that is practised during relaxation. If the imagery has been effective in producing 'good feelings' during relaxation then its use at this time should elicit similar states. This possibility is dependent upon the athlete having practised and learned the skills of positive imagery to the extent that there is a bond established between the athlete's feelings and the imagery.

6. Athletes should consider increasing their arousal level immediately before performance. This is often called 'pumping-up'. The purpose behind it is to increase the level of concentration on the initial aspect of the performance and to allow the slightly increased level of arousal to be channelled into the activity. This is a standard preparatory procedure for weight and power lifting and appears to work well in other sporting situations where it has been tried (swimming, baseball, wrestling). What is required is some vigorous maximum muscular activity and stretching combined with a deliberate attempt to feel a strong emotion. The athlete selects an emotion that achieves the 'excitement' purpose. This is usually one of pretending to be fierce, angry, hating, wild or ferocious. The athlete consciously tries to 'crank-up' his/her arousal level and narrow the focus of attention to the introductory stages of the contest.

Pre-competition strategies should be determined individually by each athlete. The aim of all the activities should be to narrow gradually the athlete's focus of attention to only the task itself. Coupled with this concentration is a controlled deliberate increase in arousal level. The control stems from careful planning and a gradual building of physical activity so that at the very last moment arousal is 'peaked'. The coach's principal role is to monitor that these two purposes are being achieved in the pre-competition activities.

PLANNING STRATEGY ACTIVITIES

Figure 4 illustrates a planning sheet for the development of strategies. This has been satisfactorily used by this writer for this purpose. The 'Behaviour Description' column is used to list the preferred activities that will be followed throughout the whole period prior to the competitive effort.

STRATEGY PLANNING SHEET

Name_____   Page ___

Behaviour Description	Problem & Coping Response	Feelings & Appearance	Result

Figure 4. A strategy planning sheet that has been shown to be useful for developing both pre-competition and competition strategies.

This constitutes the primary pre-competition strategy. The detail and manner in which the behaviours are recorded will vary with each individual. They should be of sufficient detail for the coach to determine that the athlete knows what he/she will do and that it will be done in a controlled manner.

For each preferred behaviour that is described in the first column of the sheet there should be a description of the outcome of the behaviour in the 'Feelings and Appearance' column. This requires the athlete to justify each activity in terms of what it will do for him/herself. Where performance outcomes can be specified for a behaviour the performance measurement is recorded in the 'Result' column. This would be the place to stipulate the immediate goals of a segmented performance.

The 'Problem and Coping Response' column lists the alternate behaviour to be tried if the preferred behaviour does not produce the feelings, appearance and/or result that have been listed. This is the coping behaviour which is performed if the primary behaviour is ineffective. If there are one or more aspects of the pre-competition preparation process that is very difficult to control, a number of alternate behaviours should be planned. There is no need to be restricted to only one coping response.

THE CONTENT OF A STRATEGY
The decision for what is and is not appropriate for a strategy is made jointly by the athlete and the coach. The initial material is developed by the athlete. The product is then checked by the coach. If changes or deletions are to be recommended by the coach then there should be sound reasoning behind each suggested change. The changes should be made in consultation with the athlete.

LEARNING
Pre-competition strategies have to be practised and learned. They are altered throughout the practice experience. They should be employed at minor and major competitions, and in simulated circumstances. The developmental process is a learning-discovery experience for both the athlete and coach. Once the initial strategy is developed it should undergo consistent appraisal and modification as a result of the outcomes which occur with each practice. Eventually, changes become few and far between.

The length of time to learn to use the strategies depends upon the athlete's maturity, experience and motivation.

Inexperienced athletes will also record more detail on the planning sheets than will experienced athletes. Pre-competition strategies should always be taken to the competition site so that they are available for referencing if needed.

TEAM SPORTS

What has been described is very suitable for individual or dual sports. However, often the logistics of the coach to athletes ratios surrounding team sports prevent the close monitoring that is necessary for developing strategies. Unfortunately, that restriction will only decrease the athletes' preparedness to compete. It is necessary for team sports to integrate both individual and team preparations so that every player's performance can be maximized. Until this is done, the performances of teams and individuals within teams will remain highly variable because adequate procedures have not been employed to control pre-competition preparations.

A feature that was evidenced in the elite team athletes in Chapter 1 was that even team athletes like to have some warm-up time to themselves. Thus, team preparations need to integrate both individual and group activities.

REPEATED ACTIVITIES

If several competitions are contested on the one day it will be necessary to produce a 'between events' strategy as well as the one which precedes the initial competitive effort. The elements of this extra strategy or strategies are similar to, if not repetitions of, the competition site section of the pre-competition strategy.

SUMMARY

A pre-competition strategy describes the behaviour sequence up to the start of the competitive effort. There are two foci within this strategy, the activities which occur away from the competition site and the activities that are followed at the arena.

A wake-up procedure was recommended to affect the basic daily attitude of the athlete. This is to be followed by a reasonably free but planned selection of activities and events. Of special importance are rest and monitoring confidence and arousal levels. The major theme behind planning these events is not to lose touch with the awareness of the forthcoming competition. The planning of these activities serves as a method for insuring against major disruptions which could reduce the competitive performance.

The activities to be followed at the competition site are more planned and detailed than those above. The use of relaxation was suggested and the combination of competitive performance simulations and mental rehearsals for the warm-up were advocated. After the warm-up is completed the athlete should consciously increase the level of arousal and narrow the focus of attention to the competitive task. The use of positive self-talk was proposed. A final feature was an attempt to 'pump-up' to achieve more arousal while narrowing the attention focus even more to the initial stages of the contest.

The planning of this strategy requires the definition of all primary behaviours with each having an alternative coping behaviour. For every item there should be an attempt to stipulate the appearance and feelings associated with the behaviour and the result of the behaviour. Planning is part of a learning experience which requires constant modification and change based on repeated uses of these strategies.

6 Suggested Content for Competition Strategies

Competition strategies encompass all those behaviours and thoughts once a contest begins, that is, when the athlete comes under the complete control of the officials. They also include de-briefing, recovery and warm-down procedures to be followed after the contest.

The content of a competition strategy will largely be determined by the sport or event to be performed and the individual. There are a number of characteristics that underlie human performance which should be considered and adapted to the sport concerned. A major purpose behind planning a competition strategy is to develop sufficient information and mental activities to consume the time of the competition totally. This aims to maintain task-relevant concentration throughout the whole activity. The opportunity for distractions to occur is minimized if the desirable degree of attention is achieved. The other major purpose is to pre-plan activities so that stress appraisals are reduced (Averill 1973; Maier 1972; Reid 1973; Staub & Kellett 1972). If the content of a performance or series of performances is fully prepared and planned then reactions to stresses and adverse events will be minimized. When strategy content is mainly determined by the athlete and learned, then performances will become consistent and have the potential to be maximized. The content of a competition strategy has to be planned, predictable and controlled (Epuran, Horghidan & Muresanu 1970; Orne 1965). Strategies will differ between individuals.

SEGMENTING THE PERFORMANCE

Segmenting an extended performance into discrete work units, each with its own separate performance goal, has already been discussed. Each segment constitutes one unit that can be completely mentally rehearsed. As far as the preparation of segments is concerned, the principles underlying each segment should be similar. Each segment should progressively indicate the likelihood of a final goal achievement.

The understanding is that athletes will enter competition with the immediate aim of achieving the goal of the first segment without consideration for any other goal including the final goal. If a segment goal is not achieved then the coping responses of the next segment or a completely alternate segment are to be used to get back 'on-track' toward ultimate goal achievement. Some sports do employ simple attempts to re-establish a position in a contest. Rowers use 20 stroke efforts to regain some lost distance, swimmers attempt to move in the third quarter of a race, team sports put on rallying spurts in the latter part of a game. These actions are often done too late. Segmented strategies usually indicate recovery actions earlier and at more appropriate times.

TASK-RELEVANT CONTENT

A major portion of any competition strategy should involve concentration on the technical aspects of the activity, such as, skills, plays, offensive moves, defensive ploys, pacing, etc. (Crossman 1977; Moore 1976; O'hara 1977). Once again the sport being performed will determine the aspects of this task-relevant content. There should be sufficient content items developed to be able to consume at least two-thirds, and possibly more, of all the thought content of the competition. Opponent analysis, anticipation, prediction, explicit self-directions, self-technique analysis, on-going performance analysis, among other things, are the general areas of content that need to be formulated and detailed. For each item in each area the appropriate feelings, appearance and results should be determined as was done with the definition of pre-competition behaviours.   For each technical aspect there should be at least one alternative behaviour (coping behaviour) to achieve the same effect.   For segmented sports performances, there may be a number of alternative strategy segments depending upon the achievements of one or more previous segments.   Since concentration on the technical aspects of a performance constitutes most of the thought activities, it is wise not to treat this section lightly.

The most problematical features of any competitive strategy are 'dead spots'.   These are periods of non-directed thought activity which arise when an athlete has 'grown tired' of concentrating on the same technique point, the athlete has exhausted his/her list of points to concentrate on, or a very strong distractor has been vaguely attended to, resulting in the athlete concentrating on neither the distractor nor the strategy.   'Dead spots' are manifested by the athlete going blank or losing control, that is, the consistent generation of the planned thoughts ceases.   Sufficient arousal and a high degree of learning (practice) usually guard against this problem provided sufficient thought content has been planned to cover the whole event duration.

Task-relevant factors include variety, alternate ways of viewing the same concept or phenomenon, plus a procedure for recovering task-relevant concentration when 'dead spots' occur or the athlete panics.   The recovery process is usually one of a number of well-learned segments of the strategy that are strong points in the athlete's performance repertoire. These serve as re-entry points back into the concentration process for the whole strategy.

As an example of task-relevant factors, Table 4 lists the technique points summary for the sport of swimming. When each item is planned in detail and attended to intently for a number of strokes, the strategy becomes involved and varied. The variation is important as it is needed to stop an athlete concentrating on the one point of technique for too long.

There is a stage in thought control where an item is repeated so often at the one time that it loses meaningfulness and effect (Bankov 1973). Such states often precede the occurence of a 'dead spot'. Thus, it is essential to keep changing the control emphases by stressing more of the total scope of the activity rather than a very restricted number of points. It is possible to repeat the same points at different times in a strategy. The repetition will be more meaningful if the presentation or the way the point is viewed differs on each occurrence.

TABLE 4

A Summary of the Technique Points for the Sport of Swimming.

START	Pull down hard
	establish aim
	think explosion words
	do not concentrate on the gun
TURNS	swim in controlled and fast
	explode off the wall
	hard stroke and/or kick to surface but under control
	break down to pace
STYLE	arm action (entry, pull pattern, depth, finish)
	hand, arm, shoulder positions
	body alignment (streamlining)
	head position (during and after breath)
	kicking action (depth, intensity)
	breathing cadence
	symmetry of action (all body segments)
	stroke length (catch and finish)
	control (smoothness, evenness, balance)

The concentration in the competition should be such that the athlete's thoughts are constantly clear and very active. In many regards the structure of task-relevant factors is that of a check-list of points which are assessed in turn as the athlete cycles through it throughout the performance.

MOOD WORDS

Throughout a performance it is necessary to embellish the task-relevant thoughts to ensure that the kind of application that is being demonstrated by the athlete is appropriate for the performance. When an athlete is supposed to move fast, he/she should move fast. When an athlete is supposed to be powerful, he/she should move powerfully. The quality of an athlete's performance can be modified and enhanced by the content of his/her thoughts in the performance (Meichenbaum 1975).

There is some convincing research evidence to support the assertion that 'how you think is how you perform' (Meichenbaum & Turk 1975). There are good researches that show that actions are speeded-up when an individual thinks of self-commands that mean quick actions (e.g., 'faster, faster', 'whip, whip, whip'). Thus, if an athlete wants to be fast in action then he/she should think fast words while performing. If an athlete wants to be strong then he/she should think strong words at the appropriate time. The type of movement words which are thought of during a performance affect the performance.

One can consider a performance to consist of a number of 'moods'. A mood is a performance quality such as speed, strength, balance, stability, agility, persistence and power. In making a tackle, a football player needs to be agile to initiate a move, fast to the point of contact, and finally powerful to bring down the opponent. A possible set of thoughts to accompany the appropriate moods of a tackle would be: 'dance, dance, whip, whip, lunge, crush'.

In the starting blocks for a sprint race the athlete should not be listening for the gun on the 'set' command but should be thinking power words, such as 'explode', 'blast', 'rip' and focusing on the initial movement action so that when the reflex action to the gun occurs the appropriate powerful movements are made. Suinn (1977) related the successful use of words suggesting stability with biathalon competitors during the target shooting aspect of that activity with the U.S.A. National Nordic Ski Team.

Table 5 lists a variety of physical performance qualities and synonyms for those qualities. The list of like words is nowhere near exhaustive. Most individuals have their own language words which have special meanings with regard to different aspects of performance. This list is used to suggest words. When athletes 'get the idea' of what is required, they then select words and statements to use to control the mood of their actions in performance. They should develop their own meaningful statements for governing the *quality* of their performance.

The main point behind these statements is that they must have direct movement counterparts. The coach should scrutinize the performance strategy that is written by the athlete for mood statements and see that they use words which are primitive enough to cause a feeling of the movement when they are said. For example, 'flick' connotes movement speed more than does 'rapid' although both are synonyms for speed. 'Crush' is more movement suggestive for strength than is 'vigorous'.

In the development of a competition strategy there should now be a mix of task-relevant content and mood-appropriate content. Since task-relevant thoughts should occupy approximately two-thirds of the thought content, the mood thoughts should consume nearly all that remains. The strategy should mix these features to produce variety and frequency of changes that will keep the athlete concentrating on the content and its sequence. If there are not enough changes of content the athlete could lose the intensity of concentration that is required for a superior performance and experience a 'dead spot'. A number of task thoughts, a mood statement or two, more task content, mood words, etc., is a probable integration. Since the strategy will be planned in detail, the structure of this integration can be monitored by the coach. It should be remembered that the thoughts are those of the athlete. Often what is written will appear to be meaningless to the uninitiated, but will be very meaningful to the athlete and coach.

TABLE 5

Sporting Activity Word List—Suggested Synonyms.

Quality	Synonyms
STRENGTH	crush, squash, violent, solid, intense, haul, bear-hug, crunch, might, muscle, force, powerful, strength
POWER (force)	might, force, heave, impel, smash, snap, rip, blast, boom, bang, thump, thrust, explode, hoist, crumble
SPEED	fast, alert, explode, lunge, thrust, jab, rap, smack, brief, flick, whip, fling, pop, dash, quick
AGILITY	nimble, move, dance, prance, brisk, alert, quick, shuffle, agile
PERSISTENCE	crowd, press, pressure, hustle, push, squeeze, smother, lean, worry, drive, strain, trouble, continue, drag
CONFIDENCE	bold, great, going, on-plan, push, concentrate, feels good, comfortable, control, continue, fantastic, terrific, superb, beautiful, magnificent, tremendous
BALANCE	rock-hard, block, dead, solid, firm, rooted, anchored, set, rigid, hard

So far the developed competition strategy contains task-relevant items which govern what will be done, that is, the performance content. It also contains mood-relevant words which govern the quality of how the task items will be done. This distinction is fine but necessary. Mood statements are the thought control mechanisms in the competition which maintain or develop the appropriate psychological state and they serve to arouse the athlete to the appropriate performance quality when required.

POSITIVE SELF-STATEMENTS

The final thought content for a competition strategy is positive self-statements. These comprise positive statements which encourage the athlete to continue with the performance. They are very important for endurance or aversive events. These statements may be considered to be 'mental pats on the back'. They serve as positive self-reinforcement for what has been accomplished in the task.

These statements are important for use at the completion of segments or units of performance. In one sense, they are self-indications that the athlete is on-track to achieving the final performance goal. The use of these statements for this purpose should be contingent upon achieving each segment goal. It is assumed that multiple-incentives will be established for each segment so that if some goals are not achieved positive self-statements can be made for other goals. With this format, performance will continue with positive application (Barber & Hahn 1962; Kanfer & Seidner 1973). If a total strategy is planned and only single goals are established for segments, a failure to achieve a segment goal could result in a reduction in performance (Bandura 1969; Hosek & Vanek 1965). In one sense, this is an explanation for changes in momentum in various games. The importance of emphasizing multiple incentives and goals is once again drawn to the coach's attention.

Positive self-statements should also be used at critical times in a performance when fatigue is increasing, during a succession of lost points or scores, or during a monotonous period of activity (Mischel, Ebbesen & Zeiss 1973). The statements in these circumstances might also embrace persistence qualities.

COPING BEHAVIOURS

Since every thought in the performance involves directing and monitoring the performance and the athlete's function, it is necessary to plan each item. In keeping with the coping approach to problem solving, it is necessary to have at least one alternative behaviour for every primary action that is planned. These alternative coping behaviours often are strategies to recover one's performance level. For example, if concentrating on certain technique features and mood statements is supposed to produce an improvement in position in a race and it does not, then the coping behaviours would consist of technique, pacing and mood alteration which would comprise an alternative set of self-thoughts to achieve the same result. If a method of defending against an attacker is not working successfully then a switch to another method of defense would be an attempt at a coping response. Scouting reports on opponents are very helpful in determining both primary and coping behaviours.

It is possible to have two levels of coping behaviours for performance. The first is as described above. The second is to have alternative blocks of primary strategies. These have been briefly mentioned above. The second form is most appropriate for team games. If certain forms of offense are not achieving their goals then it may be necessary to cope by switching to totally new patterns of behaviours. This is obvious. However, often it is not the total pattern of offense or defense that breaks down. There is the possibility of some element (a primary behaviour) being the flaw. If this item were altered to a coping behaviour it is possible that the overall strategy would be effective.   Before a major change in strategy approach is made, that is, switching from one set of primary behaviours to another set (segment), the possibility of element alteration should be considered.   It is an established principle that changes in primary performance or control strategies have an initial detrimental impact on performance (Holding 1965).   This is expressed as the axiom that consistency is better than inconsistency.   The detrimental effects of changes in primary strategies are lessened if the alternative strategy or segment that is used is an established and previously successful mode of performance. Thus, in the learning process it is desirable to have played or performed some lesser events or games using the coping strategy as the primary strategy for that occasion.

Coping with Pain

Many sporting activities develop discomforting levels of fatigue. In sporting circles this is usually termed pain and primarily is caused by high levels of lactic acidosis. The pain of sport is analogous to clinical pain because it satisfies the criteria established by Cantela (1977). The ability to tolerate such pain is determined principally by psychological variables (Blitz & Dinnerstein 1968). In fatiguing events, better athletes generally know at what stage they become stressed by the pain or discomfort of fatigue. Individuals can cope with this pain better if they are aware of its severity and the sensations which accompany it, if they are willing to recognize when it will occur, and if they have a strategy for handling it when it does occur (Meichenbaum & Turk 1975). This contrasts markedly with a common sporting approach of trying to ignore the existence of discomfort which is less effective (Gelfand 1964) but still better than nothing.

Dr Donald Meichenbaum of the University of Waterloo described four necessary phases for coping with the onset of pain. These should be incorporated into the performance strategy at the appropriate place.

1. *Preparing for the pain.* Statements should be developed which suggest that the individual will be able to handle the pain phase. For example:
   'You have developed a plan to handle the fatigue.'
   'Start to concentrate on your technique details.'
   'You have lots of different strategies to call on.'
   'The others will be hurting just as much as you but you have a strategy.'
   'You will be able to perform better than the others now because you have a strategy.'
2. *Confronting and handling the pain.* These statements initiate the sequence of events for tolerating the discomfort.

For example:
'You will tolerate this.'
'Go through each strategy item intently.'
'Thinking of strategies is more important than thinking about pain.'
'The pain is a cue to concentrate harder than you ever have before.'
'This is the signal to focus on performance efficiency.'

3. *Coping with pain feelings at critical moments.* An awareness of fatigue sensations periodically emerges during the performance and could serve as a distractor. These sensations need to be handled and the athlete's attention re-focused back onto the task. For example:
'Tiredness is a sign to work on (technique point).'
'What do I do? I start with point 1.'
'Sure it hurts, but you can manage it if you concentrate on technique.'
'Use your strategy. It will help you to keep control.'
'As the pain mounts switch to the alternative strategy.'

4. *Reinforcing self-statements.* After the stressful activity has ceased, some self-appraisal of the coping strategy should be made. For example:
'Concentrating on technique really helped.'
'You can even do better next time.'

A number of points are of interest in the above examples. The statements are expressed in the second person to give the impression of external, objective control. The use of the first person too quickly opens the door for self-oriented statements and the resultant inappropriate focus of attention (Staub & Kellett 1972). The focus of attention is on cues (task-relevant) which are associated with the performance. The concentration on task factors ('associative imagery') serves as a distraction which 'closes the gate' and will not let pain sensations be recognized. There is another form of concentration distraction called 'dissociative imagery'. In that form the concentration is on a factor not associated with performance. Such things as singing songs, working math problems and fantasizing running beside a shaded bubbling river are sets of intent imagery which also 'close the gate'. Associative imagery is used in competition by the best athletes (Moore 1976). Lesser athletes often use dissociative imagery as a distraction from fatigue. It is recommended that athletes develop only associative distractions for competition. Dissociative imagery, when mixed with associative imagery, is acceptable for training as it offers variation that wards off boredom.

PSYCHOLOGICAL INTENSIFICATION

When athletes are performing in non-fatigued states and the skills they are performing are well-learned, specific motor skill task-relevant thoughts will decrease the efficiency of the skill through the phenomenon of cognitive interference (Fitts & Posner 1967). When performing in non-stressful circumstances it is best to have the athlete not think of skill technique factors. Thus, at the start of races and games the performance strategy content is on performance mood statements and performance monitoring (pacing, effort levels, positioning, reading defenses, etc.). In the initial stages of performance, the skilled movement patterns that are performed are those which are the strongest conditioned behaviours, that is, those which are done automatically. At that time the amount of effort put into controlling the thought processes for technique-oriented content is relatively low. However, as fatigue starts to accrue there occurs a reduction in movement efficiency. This gradually worsens to the point that in heavy fatigue, movements are neither smooth nor efficient and exhibit little semblance of control because of the recruitment of many unnecessary muscles to perform the actions in question.

To avoid this rapid loss of skill efficiency, it is necessary to introduce some cognitive control of the skilled action. The amount of control is roughly inversely proportional to the loss in performance efficiency. The first signal of any uncomfortable feeling with regard to performance is the cue to introduce task-relevant thoughts of technique. This cognitive control helps to maintain the form and function of the skill and retards the loss of efficiency. It is usually required at an earlier stage in the performance than most athletes realize. It would be best to err on the side of introducing technique control thoughts too early than leaving them too late.

As fatigue heightens so should the *intensity* of thought control content. The principle, the more one is fatigued the more one has to control thinking, supports this concept. The increase in thought intensity is necessary to combat the increase in pain. When pain is high, the associative thinking content has to be very intent to maintain control and not succumb to the level of discomfort that could be recognized. There is a corresponding change in mood concentration as fatigue rises. Persistence and positive self-statements increase in emphasis as the stress increases.

A performance that starts with a perfectly rested athlete and finishes with total exhaustion, requires two modifications to the performance strategy as it progresses. First, the introduction of skill related thoughts is withheld until skill performance starts to decline in efficiency. Second, the intensity and density of thought content increases proportionally with the increase in fatigue. This directly affects the type of mood statements that are included as the performance progresses. Their content should evidence the change in emphasis that is warranted.

LEARNING COMPETITION STRATEGIES

As with pre-competition strategies, practice of the competition strategy in a variety of conditions is necessary so that the athlete can learn both the primary and coping performance strategies. These strategies are the content of mental rehearsal. It is wise to spend about one-fifth of the learning time on the coping strategy. The principles behind learning them are similar to those of learning the pre-competition strategy and they are written on the same 'Strategy Planning Sheet'.

A first attempt at planning a competition strategy should be very detailed and should include, verbatim, the thoughts that are to be used in the performance. For long duration events the strategy will be very long. A reduction in volume can be achieved by indicating repetitions of previous thinking. However, there is no avoiding the fact that long activities will require long periods and large amounts of preparation. With subsequent uses and alterations of the strategy, the content will be mastered as well as refined. Since these strategies have been used mainly in the sport of swimming in Canada, it has been noted that after 1½ to 2 years of use, newly written strategies are much more brief and conceptual in content than the original attempts. Athletes learn all the details of a feature, for example, arm positioning, control and action, and the single word 'arm' is all that is necessary to produce a very detailed and extensive repertoire of thought patterns concerning the use of arms in swimming. Consequently, the strategy of an athlete who is experienced in developing strategies appears to be quite brief when written down but in actuality remains very detailed when interpreted cognitively. There is every reason to believe that a similar phenomenon will occur with other sports when strategy development is employed over a period of time.

Every athlete, no matter how experienced, when starting to learn to formalize the development of competition strategies, must go through all the learning stages. As was indicated earlier, the learning process is very extended and no athlete should ever reach a stage of complete satisfaction with the developed product.

STRATEGY EVALUATION (DE-BRIEFING)

Performance strategies serve as a focal point for assessing an athlete's performance. Appropriate adjustments to a strategy should be made while they are still fresh in an athlete's mind. Assessments of when more pain can be tolerated, how well concentration was maintained, any improvements in the pre-competition strategy, what was planned for but not done, and the occurrence of 'dead spots' or attention to distractors should be made. The best time to perform this modification is as soon after the performance as is possible and reasonably comfortable. Both primary and coping strategies are continually refined. Their influence on performance is not likely to be noticed until the athlete has become skilled in maintaining his/her focus of attention on the performance strategies while competing. The post-performance evaluation procedure is necessary to derive the maximum benefits of psychological control (Averill 1973).

SUMMARY

Competition strategies formulate the total thought and decision-making activity of the athlete for a contest. This approach to competition will minimize the athlete's reactions to stresses and disruptions.

Strategies are segmented, if necessary, into mini-strategies which encompass their own immediate goal, a succession of which leads to the final performance outcome. The content of the competition strategy is at least two-thirds task-relevant thoughts. The other third comprises the use of mood words to maintain the appropriate psychological state and positive self-statements. These items have coping behaviours developed for them. The main problem with strategy use is the occurrence of 'dead spots'.

As a performance progresses and fatigue begins to build, there is a need for a corresponding increase in the intensity of thought content and control. This serves to maintain performance efficiency and also to block physical distractors such as pain and fatigue. The emphasis on cognitive control of skilled actions also increases in similar proportions.

Competition strategies have to be learned. As the learning process progresses there are changes in the way athletes record the strategies and their meaningfulness to the individual.   The most important feature of learning is the adjustment of the strategy as soon as possible after performance through a debriefing process.

7 Mental Rehearsal

Mental rehearsal is an essential part of an elite athlete's preparation for competition. It constitutes the imagination of a motion, series of motions, situation, or series of events. The reason why mental rehearsal is beneficial is because when an action is imagined impulses are produced which travel the nervous patterns associated with that action. This is known as the 'Carpenter effect' (Ulich 1967). Its benefit to performers is that the stimulation does facilitate the neurological patterns which produce an increase in the efficiency of subsequent imaginings or actions if they were performed. This occurs even if the stimulation is not intense enough to cause observable actions (Fujita 1973). Repeated trials and sessions of mental rehearsal also increase the performance levels of what is rehearsed, that is, it is possible to learn or at least increase the efficiency of what is already learned through mental practice (Prather 1973).

Mental rehearsal is more effective with elite or highly skilled athletes than it is with beginners or less-trained individuals (Clark 1960; Decaria, 1977). The skills and behaviours that are rehearsed should be conceptually well-established in an athlete's repertoire. This means that established skills, when rehearsed, are practised consistently, that is, the neurological patterns are stimulated repeatedly. This contrasts with the athlete who has not learned a skill to a reasonably high level. The neutral patterns which are stimulated would vary between repetitions. This produces the possible problem of rehearsing errors which could interfere with future performances as well as increasing the likelihood of increased performance variation.

Mental rehearsal is not a substitute for active practice, although the difference in effects diminishes the finer the skill to be performed (Ulich 1967). It can be used to augment practice and is more effective than observational training (learning by watching). It is most likely that athletes who train and consistently perform mental rehearsal of the many activities associated with their sport will achieve higher levels of performance than athletes who only train.

Mental rehearsal is beneficial for pre-competition and some competition activities. The majority of the research that has involved the performance of short-duration physical skills, for example, shooting a basket, doing a sit-up, throwing a ring. However, it has been shown that the mental rehearsal of complex and extended duration events also benefits the performance of what has been rehearsed (Prather 1973; Rushall 1970). This means that it is helpful to imagine whole races, downhill ski-runs, set-plays to be performed in a game, etc. This action was indicated as a pre-performance activity of elite athletes in Chapter 1.

WHEN TO REHEARSE MENTALLY
There are a number of occasions when mental rehearsal is useful.

1. When a skill or series of actions are performed competently (consistently), the imagination of those events can be used as a valuable addition to training. Thus, while injured, in travel, or not in practice time would be appropriate opportunities to do this activity.
2. The mental rehearsal of a forthcoming event is part of the advisable procedure for a competition strategy. It constitutes a motion pattern which prepares the athlete for the active performance of a task in a more or less suitable manner.

3. Mental rehearsal should be the last athlete-controlled activity to be performed prior to performing the competitive skill. Often it is embellished with emotional arousal. This narrows the athlete's focus of attention further so that heightened arousal can be used productively.

4. For many events which require repetitive performances, for example, long and high jumping, ski-jumping, punting, serving in tennis, etc., some repetitions of mental rehearsal should be performed prior to each competitive effort. Thus, it would be included as part of the competition strategy. In activities where it is possible to perform mental rehearsal prior to the commencement of the activity, it should be done.

5. When an activity is of extended duration, mental rehearsals of segments should be performed. There should be no extended rehearsal of the total event. To rehearse a 10,000 metre run would be an unreasonable expectation. Thus, hockey players would rehearse in turn a variety of set plays, a football player would rehearse the roles that he needs to play to facilitate a series of team maneuvers to be executed in the next series of downs, a distance swimmer would rehearse her first 100 metres of swimming as well as other segments of a 1500 metre event.

The two major values of performing mental rehearsal are that (1) it prepares the body and mind for activity, and (2) it serves as the main mechanism for maintaining attentional control on task-relevant factors.

DEVELOPING CONTROL THROUGH MENTAL REHEARSAL

The scope of what is attended to in a rehearsal depends upon the activity. For predictable and repetitious events, for example, field events, swimming races, diving and gymnastics, it is possible to concentrate on the primary and coping strategy segments and behaviours. More emphasis should be placed on the primary strategy with about one-fifth of the time spent on the coping strategy.

There are events and sports which change as they progress (e.g., football, rugby, squash). The deliberate anticipation of what might occur is very difficult to formulate. This problem occurs in most team games. Game plans should contain detailed descriptions of attempts to control selected offensive actions. Similarly, set defensive plays should be developed. Where these actions have been planned, then mental rehearsal of an athlete's involvement in them is possible and profitable. The construction of a playbook is the outcome of this preparatory process. The more advanced North American professional sports, such as football, have demonstrated the value of this action.

In team games there are many unique circumstances which arise where it is not possible to predict the exact actions of opponents. For example, a defensive back in football reads the offensive alignment as indicating a number of possible moves. He would have to produce a different reaction to each of them. Situational circumstances, where a number of behavioural alternatives exist with varying degrees of uncertainty, constitute the major portion of most team games and combative sports. Mental rehearsal is still possible in these sports. When a non-activity period occurs during the contest (between plays, rounds, etc.) the athlete should cycle through all or as many as possible of the probable events which could occur. This requires an athlete to concentrate on the relevant cues and actions of the sport. His/her attention should not be diminished by noticing irrelevant cues (the audience, what is happening on the bench), by allowing self-oriented thoughts to occupy his/her span of concentration, or by attending to distractions offered by the opposition.

Mental rehearsal is one of the central mechanisms for maintaining concentration and attentional control. Lapses in mental control are remedied by coach- or athlete-directed bouts of mental rehearsal.

HOW TO MENTALLY REHEARSE

Mental rehearsal is a learned skill (Baroga 1973; Rushall 1970). An athlete needs to learn how to do it and also needs to learn the content to be included. Consequently, it requires practice, self-evaluation by the athlete, and monitoring by the coach.

Coach monitoring of mental rehearsal is important. Two convenient methods are 1) to have the athlete recite what is being rehearsed in the coach's presence, and 2) to have the athlete tape record his/her private recitation of the rehearsed imagery and give the tape to the coach. The second alternative is usually more preferable.

There are six critical features which must be followed for successful mental rehearsal to be executed.

1. The imagination should be in the performance environment. It is necessary for athletes and teams to become familiar with the new contest arena prior to performing. The relevant features, important cues, and possible distractors should be noted. If this familiarity is not developed then the imagery will not be as appropriate and a portion of the true performance time will be spent adapting to the environment rather than performing efficiently. Some activity in the competition location will be necessary before the contest (Kaufmann & Raaheim 1973).

2. The skill, event or event segment should be performed in its entirety. This principle ensures the sequencing and total perspective for the performance. The rehearsal of a high jump approach without the actual jump, a swimming dive without the subsequent strokes, and similar partial rehearsals are more of a hindrance than a help. What is established is a dissonance of certainty within the sequence. For example, the high jumper is confident and familiar with the approach (a high degree of certainty) and then switches into the jump itself which has not been rehearsed and, consequently, has

more uncertainty in it than the approach. These differences usually cause errors at the point of change from rehearsed to unrehearsed segments.

3. The rehearsal must be successful. The imagery of errors will increase the likelihood of errors. Athletes must be convinced to discipline themselves to perform only positive and successful rehearsals. Some periodic self-evaluation procedure, for example, asking oneself if the rehearsals are totally positive, is usually employed to emphasize this feature.

4. At least one rehearsal should precede a performance where possible. The actual number will depend upon the athlete. In the absence of adequate research on this topic, it is wise to instruct athletes to repeat the procedure as often as they think is necessary. The vague instruction 'You will know when to stop, you will feel right' is about the best that can be offered. In this situation one just has to trust in the wisdom of the athlete. Elite athletes will rehearse for longer periods of time than will mediocre athletes (Baroga 1973).

5. The imagined skill or event should approximate the rate of performance. When an action is performed slowly and then fast, the two repetitions may seem similar. However, the nervous patterns that are involved are very different (Fujita 1973). This difference is reflected in varying speeds of imagery. Thus, if an athlete rehearses a 'slow-motion' version of what is to be done, the neurological facilitation that results from the mental rehearsal does not occur for the desired action. Actually, a competing neural pattern is activated which could result in eventual errors. It is important to imagine the actions at the speed with which they occur in the real situation.

6. Athletes should concentrate on imagining the feel of the action. If the proprioceptive and kinesthetic cues which constitute the sensations of control of an action can be stimulated then the rehearsal is even more

effective. Elite athletes are primarily attuned to the 'feel' of their movements and so a concentration on such cues is appropriate. This form of attention differs from less effective forms such as imagining in a manner that is like viewing a film of oneself performing.

The principal point behind mental rehearsal is that it does affect the performances of advanced athletes. The main requirement is having the time to do it. It does appear to have many possibilities for use in team sports where intermittent periods of no-activity occur. As was indicated above, the correct employment of mental rehearsal must be learned (see Figure 5). A developmental program for this skill is a necessary inclusion in any sport training program.

TWO FEATURES OF MENTAL REHEARSAL

It has been emphasized that the content of strategies will vary with the sport concerned. It remains a challenge for the coach to be able to adapt and invent the applications of the concepts of strategies to each particular sport and athlete. Two features that have been observed in the sport of swimming when using mental rehearsal will be recounted to demonstrate the precision of application that is required for the elevation of elite athletes' performances.

The duration of an intended event is one of the features that must be considered when planning competition strategy content and governing the rate of mental rehearsal. Each swimming race has a planned target time which is commonly segmented into 'splits', that is, a section of the race distance is completed in a certain time. With the mental rehearsal procedure, it has been found to be helpful to have athletes time the length of each rehearsal as would be done in a race. Thus, a stopwatch is used to see that the rate and duration of rehearsal is appropriate. When the athlete reaches the stage of imagining a turn at the 100 metre mark, he/she checks the watch to see that the volume of thought activity has been sufficient to coincide with the split time that is

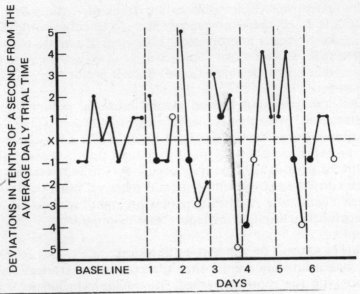

Figure 5. A balanced presentation of specific mental rehearsal and non-rehearsal procedures which illustrates the learning of the rehearsed skill. The Y-axis indicates deviations from the daily average performance of sets of four trials of 50 yards of butterfly swimming. During the baseline period of two days the time deviations ranged from +.2 to −.1 seconds. On Day 1 it could be interpreted that a fatigue factor had slowed the last trial after a warm-up effect had improved the second and third trials. A similar interpretation could be offered for Day 2. However, from Day 3 on every rehearsed trial was superior to every non-rehearsed trial. In this instance, the athlete took three days and five trials to learn the task to the extent where it was more effective than not rehearsing. The rehearsal period prior to performance was 30 seconds, the duration of the intended swim. A complete trial, dive, swim, turn and finish was imagined. The mental rehearsal of the swim improved the performance of the event. The swimmer was a world-ranked performer in the butterfly event.

desired. If the rehearsal time has been too long, then the athlete either increases the speed of the imagery, keeping in mind to approximate the race action rate, or deletes some of the informational content.   If there has not been sufficient content to fill the time period, that is, the rehearsal is completed too quickly, the athlete either slows down the rate of imagery or increases the volume of content. This timing is used for all splits and the total event time. It constitutes a method of developing precision in the imagery. In this case, the mental rehearsal is very specific to the intended action. It should be possible to use the stopwatch in this fashion for the mental rehearsal of other timed sports (e.g., rowing, canoeing, track).

A second feature that is exhibited by swimmers during mental rehearsal and should be evidenced by all athletes, reflects the intensity of concentration on the activity. It was stressed in the previous chapter that the intensity of thought control and application should increase as fatigue and/or pain increases. This increase in intensity should be evident in mental rehearsals. In the initial stages of a rehearsal, which corresponds to the lowest intensity of thought effort, there will be few overt signs of activity in the athlete. As the imagery intensifies, that is, the rate of neural firing within the athlete increases, it should become difficult for the athlete to remain passive. Movements should become very evident and the athlete will usually have to move around to complete the rehearsal. With swimmers, head and arm movements are very noticeable and they often need to walk to complete the rehearsal trial. The point behind this is that if the athlete does not display these large overt movements at the end of a trial for an activity which requires the intensification feature, then it is not being executed correctly.

The coach should expect an athlete to exhibit some bodily movements during mental rehearsal. If there are none displayed, then it can usually be assumed that the athlete is not concentrating intently enough and/or the content imagined is not that of the action and feelings of the skill. Athletes should be encouraged to exhibit these movements during mental rehearsals.

SUMMARY
As a means of summarizing this chapter the points stressed
by Baroga in his 1973 presentation will be recounted.

1. Mediocre athletes concentrate on factors other than
   performance factors (e.g., family, failures, friends,
   nothing).
2. Elite athletes mentally rehearse the exact skill in a successful manner.
3. The imagery of elite athletes has exact motor patterns
   which are of similar form and temporal relationship
   to the skill.
4. The rehearsal time is constant and longer for elite athletes whereas, it is shorter and more varied for mediocre
   athletes.
5. It is better to err on the side of doing too much mental
   rehearsal than too little.
6. One needs to train specifically for an event in order to
   derive the maximum benefit from mental rehearsal (i.e.,
   it needs to be practised and learned for each different
   event).

8   Relaxation

Relaxation procedures are useful in a number of circumstances which surround the preparations for serious athletic competitions. Their principal uses in these situations are:
1. the removal of general anxiety states,
2. the removal of localized tension,
3. the facilitation of rest, and
4. the promotion of sleep.

There are a variety of names given to and many forms of relaxation training, for example, autogenic training, progressive relaxation, active relaxation, etc. The techniques for producing relaxed states vary with the person using it and the purpose of its use. As with most psychological procedures, the techniques of relaxation need to be learned and practised.

This section will consider one method of relaxation training that was popularized by Dr Jack Turner (1972), its implementation into an athlete's training program, and the possible uses of relaxation in training competition situations.

FACTORS IN RELAXATION TRAINING

From all the varieties of techniques which involve the production of relaxed states, this writer has found one method, above all others, which appears to be more relevant and acceptable to athletes. The technique involves the active contraction of the muscles followed by relaxation. There is a physiological reason for actually 'working' to relax. When a muscle is contracted and then is relaxed, the muscle returns to a more relaxed state than prior to the contraction. When the muscle contraction is intense and isometric for a brief four to six second period, many muscle fibres contract. The subsequent relaxation promotes a high degree of relaxation in the total muscle. Consequently, the muscles of the body can better be relaxed through the use of isometric contractions in this manner. However, exercises alone will not generate all the potential effects which can be achieved with relaxation procedures. The thoughts that accompany the exercises are as important as the exercises themselves. In fact, the relaxation procedures which rely solely on thought content to produce relaxed states eventually do produce reductions in tension. Feelings of heaviness, warmth, tingles in the muscles, loss of sensation, breathing control and regulation need to accompany the exercises. The thought processes of the athlete need to be compatible with the physiological states of the muscles. Most people prefer to concentrate on only one form of feeling once they have experimented with the procedures. In training athletes to relax, it is necessary to acquaint them early with the possible feelings they could experience and let them elect to choose the feeling they prefer.

Another factor that will affect how athletes learn to relax is their motivation. Those who want to learn to relax will learn faster and achieve control much more readily than will those who do not want to participate in the program or who question the value of the process. Motivated athletes will be able to practise themselves and will probably take the training 'seriously'. Reticent athletes will require more coach-directed training sessions and intermittent re-training sessions. The coach will have to decide whether he/she can afford the effort and time required to train resistant individuals.

A final factor that is conducive to learning to relax is the atmosphere and environment where the training takes place. Quiet, very dimly lit rooms that are free from interruptions are best. The athletes should be warmly clad (long sleeves, long pant legs, socks) and should be resting on a soft surface but one that is not too soft (a gym or wrestling mat is ideal). The environment should be one that will minimize distractions so that the athlete can focus his/her attention totally on the task at hand. A number of athletes can be taught these procedures at the one time because in the supine lying position that is advocated surrounding athletes are not readily visible.

RELAXATION TRAINING

The First Relaxation Session

It should be noted that the verbal instructions given here (in italics) are for example only. For the coach to give this training session, it is best that he/she expresses the content in his/her own way.

1. Select a dim quiet room and ensure that no distractions or interruptions will occur.
2. Check to see that the athletes are warmly clad and that the clothes that they wear are dry (not damp or sweat laden).
3. Spread the athletes out around the room so that there is at least one metre between each of them.
4. Explain the principle behind relaxing:
   'Relaxation is important. What we are going to learn will help you to rest and sleep when it is necessary. To get you to relax we are going to do a set of exercises. There is a scientific reason for this because when you contract a muscle and then relax it, it returns to a state that is more relaxed than before the contraction took place. So, to get you to relax you need to do a series of exercises which contract and then relax all the muscles in your body. This first session will take about 30 minutes.'
5. *'Start in the anatomical position. Lie on your back with your arms at your side. Check these features:*

1) *the middle of your head is touching the mat so that you are looking straight up,*
2) *your shoulders are exerting equal pressures on the mat,*
3) *your buttocks are exerting equal pressures on the mat,*
4) *your calves are pressing equally on the mat, and*
5) *your heels are pressing equally on the mat.*

You should be lying straight on the mat. Your spine should be straight, your thighs and calves close together touching lightly and your arms extended by your side with your palms facing slightly up.

Check for the last time that you are straight, relaxed, and that the pressure of your body parts on the mat is equal on both sides of your body.

You most probably will find the exercises easier if you lightly close your eyes.'

The coach should then walk among the athletes to see that their position is correct. It is preferable that *no* head pillows be used and that no shoes are worn.

6. *'We are now going to do a series of exercises. Each exercise will contain a very hard contract— hold— and then release sequence. The hold is for a period of four to five seconds. Relax back to the position that you are now in. When you do the exercises only contract the muscles that are involved in them.'*

7. It is good practice to do a preliminary exercise involving the arms.

'Slowly move your arms to a position where your hands are together, fingers straight, and palms touching as if you were praying. When I say contract I want you to push your hands together as hard as you can and hold that force for five seconds. Then slowly let your arms sink back to your side as you were before.

Ready!

Contract!   Only tighten your arms and shoulders, nothing else—three—four—five—relax slowly to your side.

Feel your arms relax, they may tingle a little, they may feel heavy, they may feel warm.'

8. It may be necessary to give some pointers to the athletes at this stage.
   'During that exercise some of you tightened your legs, others their faces. Remember, contract only the part of your body that is being exercised.
   The exercise we have just done is always the first that you do.
   Let us do it again for practice.
   Slowly move your arms to the prayer position. Ready! Contract—two—three—four—five—relax and slide to your side. Feel your arms heavy, feel them pressing on the mat, relax.'

9. The exercise routine progresses from the toes to the top of the head. After the first two exercises there is an introduction to concentrating on breathing control. By the time the exercises are completed the emphasis should be on breathing control and total heaviness.

10. *'The first exercise is a toe-curl backwards. Moving only your toes and not your ankles curl your toes back to the tops of your feet. Ready, contract—two—three—four— five—relax. Let your toes go to the position that seems the most natural for them.'*

11. *'The next exercise is the opposite of what you have just done, a toe-curl under. Remember do not move your ankles. Curl your toes under your feet. Ready, contract—two—three—four—five—relax. Let them return to where they feel most natural.'*

12. This is the stage where there is an introduction to breathing control.
    'From now on when you contract do not breathe. When you relax let all the air in your lungs out so that any breathing you do after an exercise is very regular and the very minimum that is necessary. I should be able to hear you all breathe out when I say relax. After each exercise do six breaths where you concentrate

on making them even and very slight; six identical, hardly noticeable, breaths.
The next exercise is an ankle bend. Pull your feet back to your shins as much as you can. Ready! Contract— two—three—four—five—relax and breathe out. Breathe it all out, settle into a steady even breathing pattern. Do six identical breaths.'

13. *'The next exercise is the opposite of the previous one. This is an ankle stretch where you point your feet as much as you can. Ready! Contract—two—three—four— five—breathe out, even breathing.*
Feel that your feet are heavy, they may even tingle slightly when compared to the rest of your body. See that there is no tension in your toes or ankles and that your heels are pressing on the mat with exactly the same pressure. Keep your breathing even.'

14. *'The next exercise is to press your knees together. If your knees are not touching move them slowly together. Press your knees together as hard as you can. Ready! Contract—two—three—four—five—breathe-out, steady, even breaths.*
Count your breaths and make them as small as possible.'

15. *'The next exercise requires you to contract your thighs. Make your thigh muscles as small and as bunched as possible. Ready! Contract—two—three—four—five— breathe-out; steady, even breathing.*
Feel your legs heavy. The pressure on the mat should be equal behind your heels, your ankles, your thighs. Breathe evenly.'

16. *'The next exercise requires that you make your buttock muscles as small as possible. Make them rock-hard and little. Ready! Contract—two—three—four—five—breathe- out.*
Breathe evenly.
That completes your leg exercises. We have reached what is called a check point. *At this stage you go back and check each segment of your legs for the same*

feeling of heaviness, the same loss of sensation, the same pressure on the mat. If there is still some tension in a muscle group you should repeat the exercise for that group.

Check that your toes are loose.

Check that your ankles have no tension—they are hanging in a natural position.

See that your calves are totally loose.

Your thighs should feel heavy and droopy.

Your buttocks should be very soft.

Check that you have the same feeling of heaviness in your feet, your lower legs, the tops of your thighs.

Feel where your legs touch the mat. Make sure they feel super heavy where they touch. There should be the same amount of heaviness in each leg. You should feel that the mat is pressing against your legs.

Concentrate on the heavy, dead feeling. If you wanted to move your legs you could not because they are so heavy.

Do twelve even easy breaths while your legs are totally motionless.'

17. *'The next exercises concentrate on your body and shoulders. As you do these keep your legs totally relaxed. Also after each exercise do eight controlled minimal breaths.*

Press your stomach muscles into your abdomen as hard as you can. Do it so that the tips of your spine show through to the front. Ready! Contract—two—three—four—five—breathe out, let out all the tension. Concentrate on your breathing.'

(Leave sufficient time to get in more than eight, very even, controlled breaths.)

18. *'The next exercise requires you to contract all the muscles in your back towards your spine. Pull your shoulder blades together and push the points of your shoulders into the mat. Remember only contract your back muscles, do not rise up off the mat. Ready!*

*Contract—two—three—four—five—breathe out.   Let the
tension in your back go.
Breathe evenly.'*

19.   *'Now we do the opposite exercise. Compress your chest
muscles together and round your shoulder points
together.   Ready!   Contract—two—three—four—five—
breathe out. Let your shoulders slide back to the most
relaxed position.
Breathe shallow and steady.'*

20.   *'The next exercise requires that you raise your shoulders
up towards your ears; a mighty big shrug. Keep every-
thing else still, only move your shoulders.   Ready!
Contract—two—three—four—five—breathe out.   Let it
go.   Feel your body getting very heavy and losing its
sensations.
Do eight very shallow, hardly noticeable breaths.'*

21.   *'There is one more exercise to do for your body. That
requires you to pull your shoulders towards your feet.
This is done by pointing as hard as you can with your
fingers and reaching down your thighs as far as possible.
Ready!   Contract—two—three—four—five—breathe out,
relax.
Concentrate on using as little air as possible when you
breathe.'*

22.   *'That completes your body exercises. This is the second
check point.   Here you check your body and leg seg-
ments for the same feeling of heaviness, the same loss
of sensation.
Check your shoulder looseness and heaviness.
The middle of your back.
Your chest and stomach should be very relaxed.
Your buttocks very loose.
Your calves, ankles and thighs very loose.
See that the mat is pressing evenly on each side of your
body, on your shoulders, your buttocks, your thighs,
your calves, your heels.
Concentrate on feeling heavy.*

Count twelve very, very small even breaths.'

23. *'The last section of your body to relax is your head. There are many muscles in your neck and head so this is very important.*
The first exercise requires you not to move anything except to pull your jaw down into your neck. Ready! Contract—two—three—four—five—breathe out. Relax. Count those eight breaths.'

24. *'Next press your head directly into the mat. Do not arch your neck. Press directly down. Ready! Contract —two—three—four—five—breathe out.*
Since these exercises use small muscles they require small amounts of energy. Consequently, your breathing should not change much and it should be hardly noticeable.'

25. *'The next exercise requires that you jut your jaw forward as much as you can. Ready! Stick it out—two—three—four—five—breathe out. Relax your jaw. Breathe.'*

26. *'Next clench your teeth. Bite them together as hard as you can. Ready! Contract—two—three—four—five—breathe.*
Eight even breaths.'

27. *'Keeping your teeth lightly together spread your lips apart as much as possible. Ready! Contract—two—three—four—five—relax.*
Breathe.'

28. *'Press your tongue against the roof of your mouth as hard as you can. Make your tongue as big as possible. Ready! Contract—two—three—four—five—breathe out. Eight even breaths.*
Feel heavy, even dead all over your body.'

29. *'Your eyes need to be compressed as much as possible. Pull your cheeks up and your eyebrows down as hard as possible to compress your eyes back into your head. Ready! Contract—two—three—four—five—relax. Let your face go smooth. Smile slightly.'*

30. *'The last exercise requires you to make your forehead as wrinkled as possible while keeping your eyes closed. Ready!   Contract—two—three—four—five—relax.   Let that tension go right out of your head.*
Feel your face as being smooth, drowsy, very, very relaxed. Your jaw should just hang there.
Do twelve very small, slow, rhythmical breaths.'

31. *'Since that is the last exercise check once again your whole body for heaviness.*
  Your legs: heels, calves, thighs, buttocks.
  Your body: stomach, chest, lower back, shoulders.
  Your head: neck, jaw, tongue, eyes, forehead.
See that all pressure points on the mat are even and very, very heavy.
Do twelve very slow breaths.'

32. At this stage the coach can terminate the first training session. However, it is worthwhile to allow the athletes to remain in this relaxed state for five minutes or so. Some of them may be asleep.

33. To arouse the athletes be very gentle in your commands. *'After you have relaxed for a while it is important that you do not suddenly jump up. Gradually bring yourself back to normal by doing the following things:*

  wiggle your toes
  wiggle your fingers
  move your feet
  move your hands
  open your eyes very slowly
  smile
  move your elbows
  move your knees
  slowly rise to a sitting position
  move to a kneeling position
  stand
  have a good stretch

  Now you are free to leave!!'

Subsequent Relaxation Sessions

1. Subsequent relaxation sessions will be shorter in duration since explanations will be required less and less.
2. This procedure will usually take at least 15 minutes when it is coach-directed and commands are kept to a minimum. It will be shorter when it is under athlete control.
3. The aim should be to have the athletes learn the technique so that they can control themselves and relax when needed.

It should be emphasized that this procedure is just one of many procedures which exist. The contraction-relaxation action has several advantages for athletes who have been exercising and it does afford them the opportunity to gain quicker control over the relaxation process than can be done with purely passive (thought alone) techniques.

LEARNING TO RELAX

The fastest way to learn the relaxation technique described above is to do a number of sessions very close together. This differs from the normal clinical procedure where training is extended over quite a long time because there is usually only one practice session per week. A schedule of practices that has proven successful is as follows:

Day 1. First session under the coach's control.
Second session by the athlete as going to sleep.
Day 2. Third session under the coach's control.
Fourth session by the athlete as going to sleep.
Day 3. Fifth session by the athlete but in the presence of the coach and other athletes.
Sixth session by the athlete as going to sleep.
Day 4. Seventh session under the coach's control.
Eighth session by the athlete as going to sleep.
Day 5. Ninth session by the athlete during the day.
Tenth session by the athlete as going to sleep.

If necessary, further sessions can be scheduled:

Day 6.   As for day 5.
Day 7.   As for day 4.
Day 8.   As for day 5.
Day 9.   As for day 5.
Day 10. As for day 4.

The frequent coach sessions are more for motivational purposes than for teaching. They are used to stress the importance of the process and to impress that upon the athletes. The coach should periodically inquire as to how athletes are relaxing. It may be necessary to hold 'booster' sessions, where a coach-directed session is held, at varying times, to re-emphasize the uses of the procedure and in particular the imagery.

POSITIVE IMAGERY

When people are in a totally relaxed state they are very receptive to assuming new ideas and points-of-view. The situation is somewhat akin to being in a hypnotic state. When totally relaxed this receptivity can be used to advantage by the athlete. By producing positive images of themselves in a particular environment and/or doing their activity, they can be helped to enhance their own self-concepts and approach responses to the various imagined situations. Athletes should be taught to use positive imagery with the relaxation procedure.

In the initial learning phase the coach should direct and example the kinds of thoughts that should be produced. In a short while, athletes 'get the idea' of what needs to be done and if they are motivated enough will be able to proceed with positive imagery in a satisfactory self-directed manner.

Positive Imagery for Self-concept

Athletes should imagine themselves doing various skills and tasks associated with their sport. The images should have them doing the items very well and successfully. They should 'see' themselves being very satisfied with what they are doing. They should imagine enjoying the activity. These characteristics are the essence of positive self-imagery. The essential ingredients of the content are competence, enjoyment, and clear imagery. One quick way to generate initial positive self-imagery is to have the athletes recall a very successful and pleasurable moment associated with performing the activities of the sport, for example, scoring a goal, completing a difficult routine or stunt, running a good flight of hurdles, etc. Once this is developed, the athlete can imagine new situations where competence and enjoyment are obvious features.

As with any suggestion procedure, the initiative of the coach and the coach's understanding of the athlete's perspective is most important. It may be necessary to have the athlete verbalize each scene before concentrating on it. In the early sessions of self-imagery development, this verbalization is a good strategy to gain the cooperation of the athlete.

Positive imagery in an Environment

Certain environments produce anxiety in athletes. For example, a particular level or site of competition may be anxiety provoking. While in a relaxed state, if the athlete imagines him/herself in that environment doing the routine tasks associated with it, for example, in competing they would be warming-up, getting ready for competition, then competing, etc., and these tasks are done proficiently, competently and with a sense of satisfaction and enjoyment, then positive approaches will be developed towards that environment. In short, the athlete mentally rehearses the pre-competition strategy while in a relaxed state.

This approach is commonly used in behaviour therapy. For the coach, however, it is enough to have athletes work on the positive imagery while relaxed. The relaxation is incompatible with tension and anxiety so by repetition, positive associations will be linked with the environment that is imagined. This procedure is a good process to implement for all athletes prior to very serious competitions.

Positive Imagery in an Activity

If an athlete has a fear or dread of a particular skill, stunt, or activity then it is most likely that the athlete will need skilled psychological help to overcome that fear. However, when an athlete has activities that are less preferred than others, then it is possible to increase the athlete's approach response to those activities through positive self-imagery. Having the athlete imagine the specific event and concentrate on the successful and pleasurable experiences associated with it produces the positive imagery. Once again the coach's initiative in being able to induce these images will determine the success of the procedure.

Athletes should be encouraged to seek and develop positive self-imagery during relaxed states. To maintain contact with what is being pictured, the coach will have to inquire periodically of the athlete as to what is being imagined.

LOCALIZED RELAXATION

Some athletes have a need to produce direct relaxed states, that is, relieving tension in specific areas of the body. For example, one common tension spot is the neck region. If the athlete does the relaxation exercises associated with the shoulders, neck and jaw then this tension can be relieved. Similarly, 'butterflies in the stomach' can be relieved by the athlete doing the abdominal relaxation exercises that have been described above.

There is one major variation in the relaxation procedure that is usually necessary when trying to alleviate some localized tension. That variation is the repetition of the exercises. In the general relaxation procedure all the exercises are usually completed once. In this case, to remove local tension or nervousness, it may be necessary to repeat the exercises more than once. As a rule-of-thumb, the maximum number of repetitions is three. If the tension is not removed by then it may be necessary to have some external agent, such as a physiotherapist or the coach, massage or stretch the tensed area. It is a good practice that after such an intervention (rub-down, stretch, etc.) to have the athlete do the localized relaxation procedure once again so that the relieved state is brought under the athlete's own control.

RELAXATION BEFORE COMPETITIONS

Relaxation can be used in two major roles prior to competition.

If a competition is preceded by a carefully planned preparation, then relaxation can be used as the first activity of that routine. For example, two hours before competing the athlete does thirty minutes of total relaxation with appropriate positive imagery. This means that each competition preparation starts from the same arousal level (total relaxation) and with the same attitude (positive). Thus, the relaxation procedure initiates the preparation in a consistent manner. It also has the advantage of possibly dissipating tensions, unnecessary arousal, and poor self-concepts which may have arisen through situational circumstances on the day of the competition prior to the initiation of the relaxation procedure. This point has been discussed in Chapter 5.

It should be stressed that there is a school of thought that proposes being totally relaxed immediately before competing. It is recommended that this not be done as there is an extensive time period required for any athlete to prepare themselves for competition. Quite often a totally relaxed state would hinder rather than help an ensuing performance and it would be incompatible with the generation of high levels of arousal.

Relaxation can be used to heighten recovery. After a period of active recovery a rest period of concentrated relaxation would help the recovery process. It also serves to stabilize the concentration of the athlete rather than attending to distracting events. It is particularly good for use between repetitive performances such as are required in gymnastics or between heats and finals.

RELAXATION AS REST

Rest is a necessary function that athletes need to be able to perform. Rest is often required before and during serious competitions. If athletes place much importance on resting but perceive that they are not resting, then they often become worried and tense. This increased anxiety can be detrimental to performance. Athletes who have learned a relaxation procedure can use the procedure to facilitate rest and alleviate anxiety.

Often rest is equated with sleep. It should be indicated to athletes that conscious relaxation with positive imagery is as good as, and in many cases better than, sleep. Thus, the relaxation procedure is helpful for producing restful periods that are necessary for competition preparation, recovery and the athlete's well-being.

RELAXATION AND SLEEPING

Many athletes have difficulty sleeping prior to competition. For some, the interference starts days before a serious competition. Producing a relaxed state is helpful for athletes who are worried by not getting enough sleep. To remove their concerns it is often necessary and correct to equate periods of relaxation with periods of sleep.

There are a number of steps which can be added to the relaxation procedures outlined above that can induce sleep.

Some individuals do not sleep on their back which is the position assumed for relaxation. For such persons, it is necessary that they turn to their preferred position to go to sleep. This should be done very slowly and with as little effort as possible. As much as two minutes may be needed. The turning process should be one which maintains the relaxed state.

There are three foci of attention which are commonly used to produce sleep. The first is that of heaviness. The individual concentrates on the segments of the body and their heaviness. A detailed appreciation of the pressure of the bed or mat surface on each limb and pressure point is systematically undertaken. Example: 'Feel your legs weighing very heavy; the mat is pressing against your heels, . . . your calves, . . . your thighs. . . . The pressure is so great that you feel them pinned there. . . . If you wanted to move them you could not. . . . Your legs feel like lead that is welded to the mat . . . etc.'

This procedure is repeated until the individual falls asleep. It is done very slowly.

The second procedure concerns a concentration on breathing. It can be seen that this and the former procedure are just prolongations of the original relaxation procedure. The person trying to sleep concentrates on greater numbers of breaths, making each set shallower and slower. This is somewhat like counting sheep except that there are some physiological changes which result from this process.

The final procedure entails the use of controlled imagery. The athlete visualizes a bland colour that totally fills what is imagined. This is difficult to do and requires time, practice and concentration. When the imagery is one consistent neutral colour, for example, grey, buff, dusky blue, a very small dot is imagined in the center of the visual field. The athlete then slowly expands the dot for a period of two to three minutes until it finally consumes the whole colour space with total blackness. The individual should be asleep before this final stage is reached.

These are three procedures that are designed to induce sleep after the relaxed state has been achieved. Other variations do exist. If the athlete is not able to sleep after these techniques have been attempted conscientiously, then medical advice should be sought.

PRACTICE

Both relaxing and sleeping require practice. There is a skill to doing both. Consequently, the athlete and coach will have to experiment with the procedures and individual variations to produce the best process for the athlete. The development of this skill is highly individual. Some will attain it almost immediately. Others will take as many as a dozen sessions. The secret ingredient in the learning of the procedures is that of control. The athlete has to be able to focus his/her attention on the task at hand and its associated sensations. Usually, when this is achieved the process is mastered.

TABLE 6
The Suggested Sequence for Relaxation.

INTRODUCTION	1. Anatomical position. 2. Prayer position arm-push. 3. Anatomical position.
LEGS	1. Toe-curl back. 2. Toe-curl under. 3. Ankle back (dorsi flexion). 4. Ankle under (plantar flexion). 5. Knees press (together). 6. Thighs contract. 7. Buttocks contract. 8. Check for heaviness and breathing.
BODY	1. Stomach compress. 2. Shoulder points back. 3. Shoulder points forward. 4. Shoulder points up. 5. Shoulder points down and reach. 6. Check for heaviness and breathing.
HEAD	1. Chin compress into neck. 2. Press head into mat. 3. Jut jaw forward. 4. Clench teeth. 5. Spread lips apart. 6. Tongue compress. 7. Eye compress. 8. Forehead wrinkle. 9. Check for heaviness and breathing.
RESTING	1. Good feelings about sport. 2. Good feelings about self.
GETTING-UP	1. Very slowly. 2. In own time. 3. Stretch if necessary.
SLEEPING	1. Progressively reduce breathing. 2. Progressively increase heaviness. 3. Progressively increase dot on bland field. 4. Turn over slowly to preferred position.

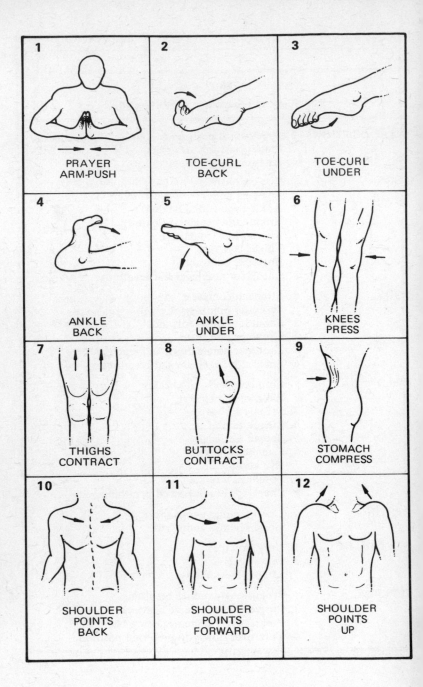

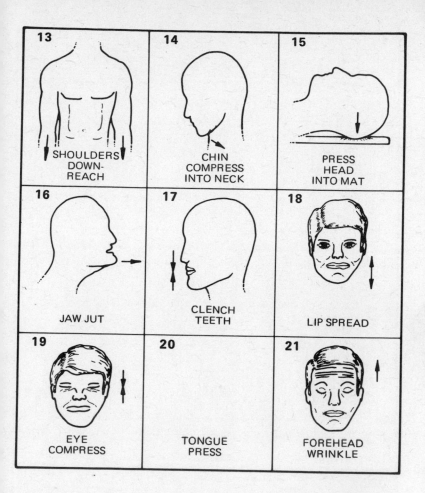

Figure 6. Suggested relaxation exercises.

This text has presented the arguments for and descriptions of the appropriate psychological processes for preparing athletes for serious competitions. The importance of developing the necessary behaviours to strengthen the psychological characteristics and behaviours of athletes has been stressed. To adopt what has been described will require some alteration in orientation to the role of coaching by most coaches. The major changes are described below.

CHANGES IN COACHING
The first adjustment of training content that needs to be developed is the inclusion of psychological content and training in the practice schedule. Teaching athletes what to look for at competitions; suggesting and role-playing coping behaviours; learning the self-evaluation processes of performance; being educated as to the criteria for self-assessment and features of performance; adopting pre-competition and competition strategy development behaviours; developing a self-awareness of arousal, anxiety and confidence control; learning when and how to do mental rehearsal, positive imagery and relaxation; etc., are only some of the broad areas which have to be added to the training program content. These additions will be more difficult than one would suspect because psychological capacities and behaviours are more idiosyncratic to the athlete than any other performance capacity. This requirement places an extra load on the coach who intends to upgrade his/her coaching performance. The first aspect of that extra requirement for more effective

coaching is to plan and document all the factors that have to
be considered for psychological preparation. This needs to
be done even before any program is attempted with athletes.
A suggested procedure for doing this is to start at the begin—
ning of this text and document each item and develop an
application of that item to the particular sport. After that
chore is completed, expand the list further by adding the
peculiar requirements of the specific sport that need to be
considered, that is, those items which have a capacity to
affect the performance of the athlete (e.g., officiating,
equipment, competition organizations, performance repetitions, etc.). This activity will serve as an avenue for coach
education and self-development. It will serve to focus the
coach's attention on the competition situation, its complexity, and its power to destroy an athlete's application to
and potential for performance. It attempts to highlight
the problems and solutions of a sport to enable an athlete to
achieve in and enjoy athletic competition.

The adoption of a psychological ingredient in the training
program is further complicated by the fact that to obtain
maximum benefits from the emphasis, the consideration of
the individual is paramount. This will require the coach to
accentuate his/her individual counselling, attention and
program prescription behaviours. This feature is of great
importance to team sports.

It has been expedient for coaches to adopt group training
approaches in the past, that is, all athletes are given the same
or similar programs, talked to as a group, and are subject to
the same developmental opportunities irrespective of their
capacities or sport-development needs. Such an approach
denies as many athletes the opportunity to improve and to
realize their maximal potential as it does to allow others to
achieve their potential. The saving feature that lessens the
severity of this accusation is the migration of athletes among
coaches. Those athletes who are not suited to a sport program
(those who might not achieve in a particular circumstance)
can travel and experience other programs and, hopefully,

find one that is better suited to them. This is an accepted pattern of athlete behaviour and it changes the appreciation of coaching to the offering of sport development programs which are suited to restricted types of individuals. The variation in coaching programs satisfies the variations in physical types of persons/athletes. This still does not maximize the developmental capacity of a coaching program. The psychological features which differ between athletes are so susceptible to influences that even when athletes have the same physiological and bio-mechanical development programs, vast discrepancies can occur in performance due to psychological factors. There is no escape for the coach from the fact that psychological training programs *have to be individualized.*

What has been presented in this text is the assertion that coaching has to be more difficult and involved than has previously been thought. For a long time, the principal content of sports training programs has involved physical training, skill development, and/or performance characteristics (play formations, rules, etc.). What now needs to be added is the cumbersome and imposing load of individualized psychological development which is at least oriented to competition preparation and performance. This emphasis could be expanded almost endlessly if one wanted to develop social, character and intellectual capacities as well. It is a burdensome requirement. No one has ever said coaching is easy. These requirements for improving the performance of athletes may require an alteration in approaches to coaching. Effective coaching may not be possible when it is restrained to the capacities of one individual coach. Perhaps a team approach to coaching athletes is now more appropriate (Rushall 1977b).

Given the restriction that a coach has to attempt psychological development for competitions for athletes, the next requirement is the construction of an implementation plan based on all the ingredients which have been logged through the procedure described at the start of this chapter. A training program needs to be planned in a manner similar to those produced for skill and conditioning programs. The psychological development program will be extensive since it is complex and learning is involved. As a safeguard, coaches should think in terms of years rather than months for the extent of adequate psychological development. The devised units of the program can then be emphasized and presented as training units and individual tasks in tandem with the more traditional emphases of training. In many cases there is no reason why the psychological features cannot be developed at the same time as skill and conditioning activities are enacted.

The production of predictable competition performances is involved and precise. It is not an effect which can be developed through a simple act of coaching. The extent of this text attests to the complexity of the task. If the coach realizes this and embarks on an adequate educational and learning program, which is adapted where necessary to individual athletes, then competition disappointments and performance variations should be reduced. The coach has to provide information, structure the environment to allow the learning of new behaviours, and develop an emphasis on the mental activity of the athlete to be able to achieve this desirable outcome.

THE COACH AT COMPETITIONS

Since the preparation for competitions will have been planned and practised, the behaviours of the coach at competitions will be altered. There will be a reduction in the amount of direction and the performance content information that the coach will need to offer. This will have to be catered to before arriving at the competition location. Three major functions should be served by the coach when at serious competitions.

1. The provision of a model who is serious about the situation, positive about and capable of handling the

circumstances, and consistent in emotional state. Thus, the behaviours of the coach should be of the same quality as those expected of the athletes. Complaints and negative appraisals of the competition and living facilities, the organization, etc., should be non-existent. Problems which do arise should be handled in a coping manner which would be similar to that expected of athletes. Emotional consistency must be displayed if the athletes are expected to maintain their singular focus of attention on the upcoming competition. Variations in coach reactivity could serve as a distractor for it would require athletes to adapt to differing moods. The seriousness of the coach should generate the impression that it is the competition that is important and for that period of time all other considerations (e.g., family, outside friends, entertainments) are of secondary importance.

2. The facilitation of the execution of pre-competition and competition strategies. The coach serves as a resource for problem solution, questions, and advice to be used by the athlete if needed. The effect of the coach in this function will be dependent upon the degree of communication and the relationship between the athlete and the coach that has been established prior to arriving at the competition. To help this function, the athlete should feel that the coach provides a fair, objective, and credible analysis of problems or questions that are raised.

3. The symbol for carrying-out the planned, predictable behaviours of strategies. The coach's presence and actions indicate to the athletes that the preparations that have been made will be enacted. Alternative modes of behaviour, doing what other athletes do, or switches in preparation approaches are not even considered. De-briefing sessions provide the opportunity for making adjustment to strategies and in that context is the only forum for making large changes to planned activities.

At the competition site the coach monitors the athletes during warm-ups and contest preparations. Of lower priority is spectating the performance. He/she provides help, for example, performance analysis, the provision of information, etc. In the monitoring process, there should be a constant evaluation of the state of the athlete for arousal and confidence. It has been found useful by this writer to ask athletes about their confidence and arousal levels even though such questions are included in the athlete's self-monitoring activities in the pre-competition strategy. The coach can implement behaviour modification procedures at the competition site to alter an athlete's confidence and arousal levels if necessary. The recognition of problems is usually a last-minute event and so the solutions need to be enacted immediately and need to elicit active behaviours in the athletes. Each problem will require different interactions and features but some general approaches can suggest the 'flavour' of solutions. Some of these are indicated below.

1. *Loss of Confidence—Failure to Cope*

SYMPTOMS: motionless sitting; lack of action; lethargic movements; unhappy appearance; isolated and withdrawn from others; answers to questions do not contain much information; reluctant to talk to the coach or others; hides away from team; does as told but without enthusiasm; unusual amount of inactivity; sickly expression; lack of attention to equipment.

COACH ACTIONS: get athlete to admit problem; make the athlete walk or exercise; while doing the above demand the recitation of various parts of the competition strategy; simulate parts of skills requiring maximum efforts; engage in maximum effort skills; have the athlete justify why he/she should be confident of achieving each of the multiple goals; re-enact parts of the warm-up; require constant vigorous activity; get back to enacting pre-competition strategy; recite positive imagery.

2. *Lack of Arousal*

SYMPTOMS: lethargic activity; lack of precision in skill attempts; absence of vigour in actions; attention to distractors; athlete admission that is 'not up for it'; deviation from pre-competition strategy; flippant actions; socializing with other athletes or persons; watching other performers.

COACH ACTIONS: get athlete to admit problem; develop vigorous, maximum activity through bull wrestles, shoving contests, forced threatening reactions (activities that require increased arousal and have some threat); perform pump-up activities; develop irritation through demands; set higher than usual standards for the enactment of warm-up items; simulate skills for the sport and have greater than usual resistances; 'pester' the athlete to work harder and harder; get back on pre-competition strategy.

3. *Too Much Arousal*

SYMPTOMS: uncontrolled activity; perpetual motion without purpose; eliminations excessive (urination, vomiting, bowel movements); scared appearance; not performing pre-competition strategy; random or unusual behaviour; stretching or warm-up activities not according to plan; periodic social and then isolated behaviours; 'panic impression'.

COACH ACTIONS: get athlete to admit problem; walk or jog with the coach and no-one else; recite preparatory behaviours; recite initial competition strategy segment; do competition preparation behaviours under the coach's supervision; mental rehearsal of initial and early segments; emphasize control in skill simulations; concentrate harder on details of skill execution; perform continual activity while mentally rehearsing.

While these problems are being 'treated' the coach should provide his/her undivided attention. This is a rule-of-thumb that must be followed. When a last minute intervention is made, the coach should remain with that athlete until he/she comes under control of the officials. The purpose of any intervention is the recapturing of the focus of attention to the planned strategy and the attainment of the optimal arousal level. Last minute interventions can be difficult. When athletes are extremely aroused it is difficult to reason with them (Zillman, Bryant, Cantor & Day 1975). It is often necessary to first lower their arousal level before offering explanations or instructions, and then seeking the appropriate arousal level after the redirection has been accomplished.

If athletes are expected to report to the coach prior to competing, then under this new scheme the coach's instructions will change from the usual directions of what to do in a performance. With the employment of strategies, instead of telling athletes what they should do in a performance, the coach asks (monitors) whether they are on schedule with their pre-competition plans, how they feel with regard to confidence, arousal and well-being. If all the answers are positive then nothing more need be said. If there is any inkling of negativism or hesitancy then the coach should immediately attempt to bring the problem under control. One of the best indexes of the ensuing performance standard is the arousal level and symptom pattern that is revealed by the *Pre-competition Psychological Checklist* (Appendix B) if it is used as a last minute evaluation, which is one of its recommended uses. This orientation differs markedly to the directive role that is in popular use. It will require the coach to exercise constraint, to be very familiar with the pre-competition strategies of the athletes, and to act a role of certain behaviours which are important because of their effect on athletes.

The adoption of a strategy-coping approach to competition will markedly change the nature of coaching at competitions.

10 Conclusions

This book has described a model of psychological coping for pre-competition and competition situations and events. That model was developed by amalgamating the characteristics of elite athletes and established psychological principles. It was proposed that coaches should develop and train their athletes to exhibit the behaviours and capacities described. This recommendation should be acceptable for coaches if they accept the model derivation process as being valid. Coaches do emphasize copying the training programs and mimicking the technique points of the best athletes as a method for improving athlete performance. It should be just as valid to accept the psychological patterns and behaviours that are exhibited by the same calibre athletes. Frequent stress was placed on the adaptation of the model to individual capacities and competition circumstances. This feature should never be ignored.

A second proposition was to elevate psychological training to at least similar emphasis to that afforded conditioning and skill development. The psychological realm is the most involved and difficult to understand and implement. A strong case can be made for a most important status among the scientific concentrations of sports training. In the international sports scene of today, there is a consensus of opinion that the psychology of competition preparation and performance is the most influential factor in determining athletes' performances. The importance of psychological training is recognized; it now remains to be emphasized.

The underlying theme of this text was one of 'minimizing

the chances of failure', a concept attributed to David Forbes, the 1972 Olympic Champion in yachting. Indeed, the control of the many minor details that affect performance in varying strengths is an orientation which is paying dividends when it is conscientiously implemented. Pre-competition and competition strategies attempt to attend to many of the influential variables which exist on the day of competition.

A number of problem areas which could affect an athlete's preparation for competition were presented early in the text. Statements were made about *what* had to be done to remove each problem but *how* this was to be done was not indicated in most cases. It now remains to re-consider those problems to see if what was presented in the preceding chapters can be used to provide solutions for them.

Ways to Eliminate Anxiety

1. Concentration on external and task-oriented factors. The athlete should follow the physical activities and mental rehearsal features of both the pre-competition and competition strategies.

2. Relaxation sessions incorporating positive mental imagery. A method for achieving a relaxed state which is incompatible with anxiety was described. Three types of positive mental imagery were discussed which should allow the coach to direct the athlete as to what should be imagined so that the procedure will be most effective.

3. The practice of the mental content of performance prior to competition. The mental rehearsal of primary and coping strategies which are positive in their outcomes produces confidence in the performer. This effect is incompatible with anxiety.

4. The recitation and ritualization of behaviours and thoughts before competition. Pre-competition and competition strategies are learned to the extent that the athlete has practised them and is competent in their execution under stressful circumstances.

5. The production of anxiety-incompatible behaviours, thoughts and procedures as pre-competition regimens. Strategy content which produces coping responses for unavoidable aversive cicumstances, the use of multiple-goals which generates the strong possibility of at least some rewarding outcomes of performance, and the deliberate, positive approach to preparing for competition are incompatible with anxiety.

This text has provided the answers and mechanisms for removing, avoiding and/or controlling anxiety in athletes.

The Control of Arousal

1. Making athletes aware of how they feel prior to competition. The athlete-coach development of strategies, the athlete's control of him/herself in the preparatory process for competitions, the constant refinement of strategies through the process of de-briefing, and the completion of a pre-competition arousal checklist which provides feedback on the adequacy and consistency of pre-performance control, produces arousal control.

2. Recapturing previous good preparations. The de-briefing procedure focuses the athlete's attention on analyzing whether the competition preparation was or was not satisfactory. The pre-competition checklist describes how the athlete felt before the contest and, thus, provides a model of how the athlete should feel before attempting to achieve a good performance.

3. Developing consistent, predictable methods of competition preparation over a period of time. The procedures of pre-competition and competition strategy development achieve this.

This text has described the methods and processes for controlling arousal.

Attaining Attentional Control

The ability to maintain a focus of attention on the contest is maintained by following planned strategies and the thought control activities of mental rehearsal and positive imagery. The various distractors, non-verbal cues, performance expectation changes, outside distractors, and environment non-task factors are minimized by the ritualized activities of the developed strategies.

Coach Over-reactions

The emotional involvement of the coach in competition circumstances is reduced in its effects on the athlete by having the athlete prepare for a contest almost independently of the coach. An awareness of this potential problem by the coach can further decrease its impact. The role of the coach must change if he/she is to become a positive part of competition preparation.

STRATEGIES AND ATHLETES

The final question about strategies for competition is 'will athletes accept them'? The answer to this is affirmative because the concept of strategies was developed from the characteristics of elite athletes and sound psychological research. In one form or another, elite athletes attempt to develop competition plans (strategies), they rehearse them prior to competitions, and they demonstrate a coping capacity for handling stresses and emotional variations which arise in the context of serious competitions. The offerings of this text are a formalized and refined presentation of the sound psychological principles which should be used during the preparations for important contests.

As a final remark perhaps a re-counting of the experience of the 1976 Canadian Olympic Swimming Team will illustrate the degree of acceptability of the strategy concept (Jamieson, Rushall & Talbot 1976). Strategies were developed after a 2½ hour lecture and two 20 minute consultation periods in the Games training camp. This was hardly a sufficient period of time for adequate construction. Since the program was voluntary, and some coaches encouraged their athletes not to participate in the program, 26 athletes attempted to use strategies. Several of the points indicated in this text were stressed when formulating the concepts and content of the strategies. The experience nowhere near approximated a fair test of the value and acceptability of strategies as outlined in this book.

The effect of strategies on race preparation. Eleven of fourteen male swimmers considered that the formulation of race strategies was beneficial to their race preparation even though the preparation phase was not emphasized. Eight of ten females considered them to have a similar effect. This was an acceptance rate of 79% which is surprisingly good considering the limited opportunities for development, refinement and the absence of real practice.

The effect of strategies on race performance. A similar 79% rate of acceptance to that of the preparation effect was indicated. It appeared that given the limitations of the Olympic implementation of strategy development, swimmers considered their employment to be beneficial to both performance and preparation.

This brief account of a 'worst case' application still produced highly satisfactory levels of acceptance even in an area (preparation) that was not emphasized. One is set to wondering what would have been the effect if there had been sufficient time for and unanimous acceptance of their use.

Strategy development is a direction for enhancing athletic performance consistency. It formalises the characteristics and activities of elite athletes to the point where they should benefit from the conceptual clarity and directions of its components. Coaches who are committed to athletic excellence should adopt the development of pre-competition and competition strategies for serious competitions.

References

Aderman, D., Bryant, F. B. & Domelsmith, D. E. 'Prediction as a means of inducing tolerance', *Journal of Research in Personality*, 1978, 12, 172-178.

Andrew, J. 'Coping style, stress-relevant learning and recovery from surgery', *Dissertation Abstracts*, 1968, 28, 1182-B.

Atkinson, J. W. & Reitman, W. R. 'Performance as a function of motive strength and expectancy of goal achievement', *Journal of Abnormal and Social Psychology*, 1956, 53, 361-366.

Averill, J. R. 'Personal control over aversive stimuli and its relationship to stress', *Psychological Bulletin*, 1973, 80, 286-303.

Bandura, A. *Principles of behaviour modification.* New York: Holt, Rinehart and Winston, 1969.

Bankov, M. 'The hypnotic triad', in *Proceedings of the 3rd World Congress of the International Society of Sports Psychology: Volume 2.* Madrid: Instituto Nacional de Educación Física y Deportes, 1973.

Barber, T. X. & Hahn, K. W. 'Psychological and subjective responses to pain producing stimulation under hypnotically-suggested and waking imagined "analgesia",' *Journal of Abnormal and Social Psychology*, 1962, 65, 411-418.

Baroga, L. 'Influence on the sporting result of the concentration of attention process and time taken, in the case of weightlifters', in *Proceedings of the 3rd World Congress of the International Society of Sports Psychology: Volume 3.* Madrid: Instituto Nacional de Educación Física y Deportes, 1973.

Barry, G. S. 'The relationship of pre-match arousal assessments to self-perceived performance competencies in collegiate wrestlers', M. Sc. thesis, Lakehead University, 1979.

Blitz, B. & Dinnerstein, A. J. 'Effects of different types of instruction on pain parameters', *Journal of Abnormal Psychology*, 1968, 73, 276-280.

Bobey, M. J. & Davidson, P. O. 'Psychological factors affecting pain tolerance', *Journal of Psychosomatic Research*, 1970, 14, 371-376.

Botterill, C. 'Goal setting and performance on an endurance task', a paper presented at the Canadian Association of Sports Sciences Conference, Winnipeg, September, 1977.

Cautela, J. R. 'The use of covert conditioning in modifying pain behaviour', *Journal of Behaviour Therapy and Experimental Psychiatry*, 1977, 8, 45-52.

Clark, L. V. 'Effect of mental practice on the development of certain motor skills', *Research Quarterly*, 1960, 31, 560-569.

Clark, R. D. 'Group induced shift towards risks', *Psychological Bulletin*, 1971, 76, 251-270.

Coles, M. G. H., Herzberger, S. D., Sperber, B. M. & Goetz, T. E. 'Physiological and behavioral concomitants of mild stress: the effects of accuracy of temporal information', *Journal of Research in Personality*, 1975, 9, 168-176.

Crossman, J. 'The effects of cognitive strategies on the performance of athletes', M. Sc. thesis, Lakehead University, 1977.

Decaria, M. D. 'The effect of cognitive rehearsal training on performance and on self-report of anxiety in novice and intermediate female gymnasts', *Dissertation Abstracts International*, 1977, 38(1-B), 351.

Dermer, M. & Berscheid, E. 'Self-report of arousal as an indicant of activation level', *Behavioural Science*, 1972, 17, 420-429.

Dimitrova, S. 'Dependence of voluntary effort upon the magnitude of the goal and the way it is set in sportsmen',

International Journal of Sport Psychology, 1970, **1**, 29-33.

Easterbrook, J. A. 'The effect of emotion on cue utilization and the organization of behaviour', *Psychological Review*, 1959, **66**, 83-101.

Epuran, M., Horghidan, V. & Muresanu, I. 'Variations of psychical tension during the mental preparation of sportsmen for contest', in *Contemporary Psychology of Sport*, G. S. Kenyon (ed). Chicago: The Athletic Institute, 1970.

Erez, M. 'Feedback: A necessary condition for the goal setting—performance relationship', *Journal of Applied Psychology*, 1977, **62**, 624-627.

Fenz, W. D. 'Arousal and performance of novice parachutists to multiple sources of conflict and stress', *Studia Psychologica*, 1974, **16**, 133-144.

Fenz, W. D. & Jones, G. B. 'Individual differences in physiologic arousal and performance in sport parachutists', *Psychosomatic Medicine*, 1972, **34**, 1-8.

Fiorini, A. 'The relationship of pre-game arousal assessments to self-perceived performance competencies in male collegiate basketball players', M. A. thesis, Lakehead University, 1978.

Firth, P. A. 'Psychological factors influencing the relationship between cardiac arrythmia and mental load', *Ergonomics*, 1973, **16**, 5-16.

Fitts, P. M. & Posner, M. I. *Human Performance*. Belmont: Brooks/Cole, 1967.

Flexibrod, J. J. & O'Leary, K. D. 'Effects of reinforcement on children's academic behavior as a function of self-determined and externally imposed contingencies', *Journal of Applied Behavior Analysis*, 1973, **6**, 241-250.

Forward, J. & Zander, A. 'Choice of unattainable group goals and effects on performance', *Organizational Behavior and Human Performance*, 1971, **6**, 184-199.

Fujita, A. 'An experimental study on the theoretical basis of mental training', in *Proceedings of the 3rd World Congress of the International Society of Sports Psychology:*

Abstracts. Madrid: Instituto Nacional de Educación Física y Deportes, 1973.

Gelfand, S. 'The relationship of experimental pain tolerance to pain threshold', *Canadian Journal of Psychology*, 1964, 18, 36-42.

Genov, F. 'The nature of the mobilization readiness of the sportsman and the influence of different factors upon its formation', in *Contemporary Psychology of Sport*, G. S. Kenyon (ed). Chicago: The Athletic Institute, 1970. (a)

Genov, F. 'Peculiarity of the maximum motor speed of sportsmen when in mobilized readiness', in *Contemporary Psychology of Sport*, G. S. Kenyon (ed). Chicago: The Athletic Institute, 1970 (b)

Goldfried, M., Decenteceo, E. & Weinberg, L. 'Systematic rational restructuring as a self-control technique', *Behavior Therapy*, 1974, 5, 247-254.

Harris, V. A. & Katkin, E. S. 'Primary and secondary emotional behavior. An analysis of the role of autonomic feedback on affect, arousal, and attribution', *Psychological Bulletin*, 1975, 82, 904-916.

Highlen, P. S. & Bennett, B. B. 'Differences between qualifying and non-qualifying elite wrestlers: Suggested training strategies', unpublished paper, Faculty of Physical Education, University of Western Ontario, 1978.

Holding, D. H. *Principles of training*. London: Pergamon Press, 1965.

Hollandsworth, J. G., Jr., Glazeski, R. C. & Dressel, M. E. 'Use of social skills training in the treatment of extreme anxiety and deficient verbal skills in the job-interview setting', *Journal of Applied Behavior Analysis*, 1978, 11, 259-269.

Hosek, V. & Vanek, M. 'The influence of success and failure on the resulting mental activity of sportsmen', in *Psicologia dello Sport*, F. Antonelli (ed). Rome: Federazione Medico Sportavia Italiana, 1965.

House, W. C. 'Performance expectancies and effect associated with outcomes as a function of time perspective', *Journal of Research in Personality*, 1973, 7, 277-288.

House, W. C. 'Effect of locus of control, expectancy confirmation–disconfirmation, and type of goal on causal attributions of failure', *Journal of Research in Personality*, 1976, **10**, 279-292.

Jamieson, J., Rushall, B. S. & Talbot, D. 'Psychological and performance factors of Canadian Olympic Games Swimmers–1976', Research Report. Ottawa: Canadian Amateur Swimming Association, 1976.

Kanfer, F. & Seidner, M. 'Self-control factors enhancing tolerance of noxious stimulation', *Journal of Personality and Social Psychology*, 1973, **25**, 381-389.

Kaufmann, G. & Raaheim, K. 'Effect of inducing activity upon performance in an unfamiliar task', *Psychological Reports*, 1973, **32**, 303-306.

Kazdin, A. E. 'Covert modeling, model similarity, and reduction of avoidance behavior', *Behavior Therapy*, 1974, **5**, 325-340.

Kovatchev, I. 'Psychosomatic method of activating psychical functions', in *Proceedings of the 3rd World Congress of the International Society of Sport Psychology: Abstracts.* Madrid: Instituto Nacional de Educación Física y Deportes, 1973.

Levy, R. L. 'Relationship of an overt commitment to task compliance in behaviour therapy', *Journal of Behavior Therapy and Experimental Psychiatry*, 1977, **8**, 25-29.

Locke, E. A. 'The relationship of intentions to level of performance', *Journal of Applied Psychology*, 1966, **50**, 60-66.

Locke, E. A. & Bryan, J. F. 'Cognitive aspects of psychomotor performance: The effects of performance goals on level of performance', *Journal of Applied Psychology*, 1966, **50**, 286-291.

Lupfer, M. & Jones, M. 'Risk taking as a function of skill and chance orientation', *Psychological Reports*, 1971, **28**, 27-33.

Magnusson, D. & Ekehammar, B. 'Similar situations–similar behaviors? A study of the intra-individual congruence between situation perception and situation reactions', *Journal of Research in Personality*, 1978, **12**, 41-48.

Maier, N. R. 'Effects of training on decision making', *Psychological Reports*, 1972, **30**, 159-164.

Meichenbaum, D. 'Toward a cognitive theory of self-control', in *Consciousness and self-regulation: Advances in Research*, G. Schwartz and D. Shapiro (eds.). New York: Plenum Press, 1975.

Meichenbaum, D. & Turk, D. 'The cognitive-behavioral management of anxiety, anger and pain'. Paper presented at the Seventh Banff International Conference on Behavior Modification, 1975.

Mischel, W. 'Toward a cognitive social reconceptualization of personality', *Psychological Review*, 1973, **80**, 252-283.

Mischel, W., Ebbesen, E. B. & Zeiss, A. R. 'Selective attention to the self: Situational and dispositional determinants', *Journal of Personality and Social Psychology*, 1973, **27**, 129-142.

Moore, K. 'Watching their steps', *Sports Illustrated*, 1976, **44**, 81-90.

O'hara, T. J. 'A demonstration of the relationship between cognitive experience and performance debilitation in high evaluation conditions', in *Human performance and behavior*, B. A. Kerr (ed.). Proceedings of the 9th Canadian Psychomotor Learning and Sport Psychology Symposium, Banff, 1977.

Orne, M. 'Psychological factors maximizing resistance to stress with special reference to hypnosis', in *The quest for self-control*, S. Klausner (ed.). New York: Free Press, 1965.

Pollard, W. E. & Mitchell, T. R. 'Decision theory analysis of social power', *Psychological Bulletin*, 1972, **78**, 433-446.

Prather, D. C. 'Prompted mental practice as a flight simulator', *Journal of Applied Psychology*, 1973, **57**, 353-355.

Reid, L. D. 'Process of fear reduction in systematic desensitization: An addendum to Wilson and Davidson (1971)', *Psychological Bulletin*, 1973, **79**, 107-109.

Rushall, B. S. 'Some applications of psychology to swimming', *Swimming Technique*, 1970, 7, 71-82.

Rushall, B. S. 'Applied psychology of sports', in *The status of psychomotor learning and sport psychology research*, B. S. Rushall (ed.). Thunder Bay: Sport Science Associates, 1975.

Rushall, B. S. 'The scope of psychological support services for Canadian Olympic athletes', *Canadian Journal of Applied Sport Sciences*, 1977, 2, 43-47. (a)

Rushall, B. S. 'The team approach to the coaching of athletes', in *Proceedings of the Post Olympic Coaching Symposium*, J. Taylor (ed.). Ottawa: Coaching Association of Canada, 1977. (b)

Rushall, B. S. 'Environment specific behavior inventories: Developmental procedures', *International Journal of Sport Psychology*, 1978, 9, 97-110. (a)

Rushall, B. S. 'Psychological characteristics of Canadian Commonwealth Games Swimmers', Research Report. Ottawa: Canadian Amateur Swimming Association, 1978. (b)

Rushall, B. S. & Garvie, G. 'Psychological characteristics of Canadian Olympic and non-Olympic freestyle wrestlers'. ERIC Clearinghouse on Teacher Education, Washington, No. SP012-051-ED150117, 1978.

Rushall, B. S., Jamieson, J. & Talbot, D. 'Psychological characteristics of Canadian Olympic Games swimmers', Research Report. Ottawa: Canadian Amateur Swimming Association, 1977.

Rushall, B. S. & Siedentop, D. *The development and control of behavior in sports and physical education.* Philadelphia: Lea & Febiger, 1972.

Ryan, E. D. 'Relationship between motor performance and arousal', in *Contemporary Readings in Sport Psychology*, W. P. Morgan (ed.). Springfield: Charles C. Thomas, 1970.

Schulman, M. 'Expectancies as cues for predicting the reaction to failure', *The Psychological Record*, 1972, 22, 267-276.

Schwartz, R. & Gottman, J. A. 'A task analysis approach to clinical problems: A study of assertive behavior'. Unpublished manuscript, Indiana University, 1974.

Singer, R. N. 'Motivation in sport', *International Journal of Sport Psychology*, 1977, 8, 1-21.

Staub, E. & Kellett, D. S. 'Increasing pain tolerance by information about aversive stimuli', *Journal of Personality and Social Psychology*, 1972, 21, 198-203.

Suinn, R. 'Easing athletes' anxiety at the Winter Olympics', *Physician and Sports Medicine*, 1977, 5, 88-92.

Turner, A. J. *Relaxation*. Huntsville, Alabama: Cybersystems, 1972.

Ulich, E. 'Some experiments on the function of mental training in the acquisition of motor skills', *Ergonomics*, 1967, 10, 411-419.

Vanek, M. & Cratty, B. J. *Psychology and the superior athlete*. London: Collier-Macmillan, 1970.

Vestewig, R. 'Cross-response mode consistency in risk-taking as a function of self-reported strategy and self-perceived consistency', *Journal of Research in Personality*, 1978, 12, 152-163.

Wankel, L. M. & McEwan, R. 'The effect of privately and publicly set goals upon athletic performance', a paper presented at the International Congress of Physical Activity Sciences, Quebec City, 1976.

Whiting, H. T. A. *Acquiring ball skills*. London: G. Bell and Sons, 1969.

Wine, J. 'Test anxiety and direction of attention', *Psychological Bulletin*, 1971, 76, 92-104.

Wolff, B. B., Krasnegor, N. A. & Farr, R. S. 'Effect of suggestion upon experimental pain response parameters', *Perceptual and Motor Skills*, 1965, 21, 675-683.

Zillman, D., Bryant, J., Cantor, J. R. & Day, K. D. 'Irrelevance of mitigating circumstances in retaliatory behavior at high levels of excitation', *Journal of Research in Personality*, 1975, 9, 282-293.

Appendices

A Pre-competition and Competition Behaviour Inventory

This appendix contains an inventory that can be given to an athlete to determine what characteristics and behaviours for pre-competition and competition exist. It is a tool for the coach to use to determine the status of an athlete with regard to the aspect of sporting experience that has been discussed in this text.

The inventory is standardized. A set of explicit instructions should be followed when administering the test. The interpretation of the results is direct. The coach simply reads the response to each question. This action provides the coach with information about the behaviours and situations which exist around competitions.

This inventory is reproduced with the permission of the copyright holder, Sports Science Associates, 376 North Algoma Street, Thunder Bay 'P', Ontario, Canada. It may be reproduced by the readers of this text as often as is necessary.

The test results are valid for a period of up to two months. Repeat the testing if a longer time period has elapsed.

PRE-COMPETITION AND COMPETITION BEHAVIOUR INVENTORY ADMINISTRATION INSTRUCTIONS

Preparation
1. Prepare the testing room beforehand so that the atmosphere is comfortable and well-lighted.
2. Supply pencils and copies of the test to each athlete.

3. Instruct the athlete(s) not to read or answer any questions until told to do so.

Administering the Test

Read the following passage to the group:

'The test that you are about to take concerns your association with this sport. The results of this test will be used to tell (me/the coach) what are the best training and competitive procedures for you. *These procedures are designed to help you perform better*. They are designed to help (me/the coach) to do a better job of coaching. It is essential that you answer this test as truthfully as possible. False answers will cause (me/us) to proceed with the wrong approach to your coaching. It is better for you not to take the test if you are not prepared to answer the test truthfully. If you are not prepared to do this you should leave the room now. (*Pause*)

Write your name and the date clearly in the spaces at the top of the sheet. (*Pause*)

Respond by circling the alternative that best describes you. If you find a question that is very difficult to answer or does not appear to be appropriate for you then do not respond to it.

Are there any questions?

You may begin. When you have completed the test bring it to me and leave the room.'

Pre-competition and Competition Behaviour Inventory

Name _____   Date _____

It is necessary that you answer each statement as truthfully as possible. False or inaccurate answers will cause the test results to indicate improper coaching techniques for you. Take your time in answering each question so that you can answer what is true for you. Circle the alternative that best describes you.

1. I enjoy competitions more than training.
    a) true   b) in between   c) false

2. I prefer to warm-up for an important contest without talking.
    a) always   b) occasionally   c) never

3. I like to have a coach with me during competition warm-ups.
    a) always   b) occasionally   c) never

4. If someone disrupts me when I am preparing for a contest, it upsets my performance.
    a) always   b) occasionally   c) never

5. I get nervous and tense before an important competition.
    a) always   b) occasionally   c) never

6. I like to be alone before an important contest.
    a) always   b) occasionally   c) never

7. I worry about the other competitors before a competition.
    a) always   b) occasionally   c) never

8. If I am troubled before a contest, I know what to do to get myself 'up' so that I perform my best.
    a) always   b) occasionally   c) never

9. I like to have my contests planned in detail.
    a) always   b) occasionally   c) never

10. I feel that it is necessary that I have a competition plan that will tell me what to do if the contest does not go as expected.
    a) always   b) occasionally   c) never

11. I can be distracted before an important contest to the extent that it will affect my performance.
    a) always   b) occasionally   c) never

12. I mentally rehearse my competition plan before contests.
    a) always   b) occasionally   c) never

13. I am able to concentrate on an approaching contest all through my warm-up, waiting, and assembling for competition.
    a) always   b) occasionally   c) never

14. During a contest, I think of how much the effort will hurt.
     a) often   b) occasionally   c) never

15. The major thing that I think of during a contest is my technique.
     a) always   b) occasionally   c) never

16. During a competition, I hold back a little so that I know I will
     be able to put in a good finish.
     a) always   b) occasionally   c) never

17. When I start to feel tired, I try harder.
     a) always   b) occasionally   c) never

18. I do not put in a maximum effort when I know I cannot win.
     a) always   b) occasionally   c) never

19. After a contest is over, I feel that I could have performed better.
     a) always   b) occasionally   c) never

20. When I am tired during a competition, I concentrate on my
     technique.
     a) always   b) occasionally   c) never

21. I would like to be able to 'psyche-out' the other athletes before
     a contest.
     a) always   b) occasionally   c) never

22. I think about my performances for a long time after they are
     over.
     a) always   b) occasionally   c) never

23. The more detailed my competition plans are, the more confident
     I feel.
     a) true   b) uncertain   c) false

24. If I fall behind in a contest, I make the situation a test for myself
     to do my best effort.
     a) always   b) occasionally   c) never

25. I worry about how much the effort for an impending contest will
     hurt.
     a) always   b) occasionally   c) false

26. I use the information and experiences gained in a contest to im-
     prove my next performance.
     a) always   b) occasionally   c) never

27. If I am too excited before a contest, I know what to do to calm
     down.
     a) always   b) occasionally   c) never

28. If I lose confidence before a contest, I know how to recover it.
     a) always   b) occasionally   c) never

29. I want the coach to go over the competition plan before the
     contest.
     a) always   b) occasionally   c) never

30. I am in bed early enough to get eight hours of good sleep before a contest.
   a) always   b) occasionally   c) never

31. During warm-up, I practise doing things that I will be doing in the contest.
   a) always   b) occasionally   c) never

32. I am on time for competitions.
   a) always   b) occasionally   c) never

33. During the final stages of a close contest, I can handle the pressure.
   a) always   b) occasionally   c) never

34. If the spectators constantly harass and talk to me, it affects my performance.
   a) always   b) sometimes   c) never

35. When a referee or official makes a bad call or decision, I accept it without making any comment.
   a) always   b) occasionally   c) never

36. If the odds are really against winning a contest, I am still able to produce my very best effort.
   a) always   b) occasionally   c) never

37. If I have a disappointing performance, I try harder and perform better in the next competition.
   a) always   b) sometimes   c) never

38. When a contest is approaching, I can completely concentrate on it so that nothing distracts me.
   a) always   b) sometimes   c) never

39. I prefer to go out and take the lead in a contest no matter how much effort is required.
   a) always   b) sometimes   c) never

40. Before important competitions, my nerves get on edge when even very small distractions or problems are encountered.
   a) always   b) occasionally   c) never

This completes the test. Hand your answers to the person conducting the testing and leave the room.

Pre-competition Psychological Checklist

This checklist indicates the symptoms of arousal that the athlete is experiencing, the level of arousal, and an estimation of his/her chances of winning. These features are assessed prior to performance. After the performance, the event result and a self-assessment of the standard of quality of the performance are made. The coach should have the following materials duplicated and formed into a booklet which can be given to the athlete to keep.

The purpose behind the checklist is to log the arousal symptoms and level for every contest. When the athlete has attained adequate arousal control there will be a reasonable amount of consistency in the pattern of symptoms which are recorded for each different performance quality. The patterns are recorded on the *Psychological Checklist Summary*.

It is very important that the athlete record this information faithfully and enthusiastically after the definitions and instructions have been understood.

Using the Pre-competition Psychological Checklist

1. Reproduce the materials including sufficient numbers of the checklist to cover one competitive season's events.
2. Meet with the athletes and explain the importance of the task and the necessary requirement for private, truthful, accurate and conscientious responding.
3. Read the definitions and clarify any questions. Practise filling-out a sheet to indicate how the athletes feel at that moment.

4. Establish with each athlete, when the checklist will be completed before the start of a competition. About 5 to 10 minutes prior to the commencement of a contest is acceptable, although longer than 10 minutes is usually too removed from the event to reflect accurately the pre-competition arousal symptoms. The completion process is quick, usually less than a minute, and does not bother the athlete if it is part of the pre-competition strategy.

5. Establish when the post-competition assessment is made. It should be done soon after the performance before the athlete interacts with other persons who might influence the self-assessment of the performance quality. It should be the last act of a warm-down routine and should be completed before and brought to the de-briefing session.

Logging the Data of the Checklist

After each competition, the coach should collect the athletes' Checklist books and summarize the data.

1. The information about symptoms should be transferred to the *Psychological Checklist Summary*, one of which is kept for each athlete.

2. The process for transferring the symptom data is to (a) locate the column which corresponds to the athlete's rating of his/her performance, and (b) place a check mark or dot in that column alongside each symptom that was marked as present.

    After a sufficient number of contests a pattern of responses may become evident. If a symptom is checked on at least 75% of the occasions of a particular performance standard it is usually deemed to be an indicator for that standard. Thus, for example, if six symptoms have been checked with a high frequency when all the performances of that standard are considered, those symptoms become the 'symptom pattern' for that level. Remember, only elite athletes who have arousal control will exhibit consistent patterns for the 'Great' and 'Good' quality events. If an athlete does not have sufficient control then few, if any, patterns will emerge. It has also been found that better performers rarely assess a 'Poor' or 'Very poor' performance whereas poorer performers do.

3. The arousal level data should be transferred to the *Arousal Summary Sheet*. Figure 2 indicates what the data look like. The means of all the categories are joined to indicate whether a linear trend exists. Elite athletes who have adequate arousal control will exhibit an increase in arousal level with an increase in performance quality.

INSTRUCTIONS TO ATHLETES
About the Pre-competition Psychological Checklist
These checklists require you to assess how you feel prior to competition. They should be completed *just before* meeting with the coach for the last time before an event or at a pre-determined time that has been established by the coach.

The information that is provided should be the most truthful and accurate that you can provide. Some of the descriptions are very personal but remember your answers will remain private, being only known to you and the coach. The reason that this information needs to be obtained is that depending on how you answer, the coach will be able to make very important last-minute coaching decisions. These decisions should help you to perform even better than you normally would expect.

What to Do
1. Fill in your name, the date and the event or game that you are about to contest.
2. Check 'yes' or 'no' for the descriptions that are provided. If you have other feelings or problems (e.g., health, emotional, etc.) that are not listed write them

briefly in the '24. Other (describe)' section. Total the number of 'yes' and 'no' responses and enter them in the spaces provided.

3. On the numbered scale indicate where you feel you are in terms of your arousal (excitedness). Note that a −10 indicates complete inactivity and lack of excitedness whereas the +10 score is an extremely aroused feeling, something like how you would feel if you were about to make your first parachute jump or you had just been involved in a fight. The zero entry is what would be normal for you. Mark where you think you would be considering how you feel by putting an 'X' on the scale line.

4. On the estimation of winning scale, indicate what you think your chances of winning are. Place an 'X' on the scale line.

5. After you compete and before you interact with anyone else, indicate the result of the competition. Also, indicate how you feel about the quality of your performance in the 'Rate how you feel' section by checking the appropriate category.

Have this information ready for your coach at those times that have been decided upon.

DEFINITIONS FOR THE PRE-COMPETITION PSYCHOLOGICAL CHECKLIST

These items should be read to, discussed and clarified with the users of the checklists.

Items

1. *Can't be bothered attitude.* The athlete cannot get excited or interested in the contest. He/she feels the competition is not important. If it were missed the athlete would not care one way or the other.

2. *Drowsy, sleepy feeling.* The athlete feels sleepy. His/

her eyelids are heavy. He/she would prefer to sit down and doze or take a nap.

3. *Feeling of being alone.* The athlete would like to have someone to keep him/her company. He/she feels unsure of what is expected of him/her or of what to do. He/she would like to have some other person there to talk to.

4. *Feeling of weakness.* The athlete feels weak all over. His/her arms feel heavy. His/her knees are hard to keep straight. The athlete feels that he/she could just crumple-up on the floor. A strong feeling does not exist.

5. *Inadequate attention to preparation.* The athlete has not had time nor been able to prepare him/herself physically and mentally for the event. This produces a feeling of 'something wrong' in the event preparation procedures and consequently the athlete has some doubts about his/her readiness to compete.

6. *Impatient feeling.* The athlete wishes the event would occur sooner than it is scheduled. The time to be spent waiting is frustrating. The athlete feels that he/she is ready to compete at the time of completing the checklist.

7. *Aggressive feeling towards others.* The athlete dislikes the other competitors. In the event that is to come, it will be this athlete that dictates what will happen. There is no feeling of friendship with or like for the other competitors.

8. *I have cried a little.* The athlete has shed some tears while preparing for the contest. The amount of crying is not important just the fact that some crying has occurred.

9. *Some shaking and trembling.* The athlete has noticed his/her hands, legs, or some part of the body shaking or trembling. He/she has been able to see the shaking occurring.

10. *Poor movement coordination.* The athlete's techniques

feel awkward and different. The activities followed in warm-up have not felt normal. The athlete is concerned about this unusual and distracting occurrence.

11. *Trouble seeing and remembering.* The athlete has occasional bursts of blurred vision. He/she cannot focus on anything for a long time. His/her mind is in a turmoil. It is difficult to concentrate on any one thing for any appreciable length of time.

12. *I have vomited.* This has occurred at least once.

13. *I have diarrhea.* The athlete has been to the toilet frequently and his/her bowel movements are like liquid.

14. *I have urinated several times.* The frequency of urination is more noticeable than usual.

15. *I have had frequent bowel movements.* The athlete has been to the toilet frequently but the bowel movements are not like diarrhea.

16. *Nervous.* The athlete feels nervous all over. Tingling, jittery feelings occur everywhere and are noticeable. It is hard to locate where the exact feelings occur.

17. *Butterflies in the stomach.* The athlete's stomach feels like it is moving or churning inside. The nervous feeling is decidedly more evident in the stomach than in any other part of the body.

18. *Lack of confidence.* The athlete feels that he/she is not prepared or does not have the ability to perform to expectations in the forthcoming contest.

19. *Do not feel well.* The athlete feels ill or slightly ill. He/she could become sick if the feeling got worse.

20. *I do not think that I will be able to perform well.* The athlete believes that he/she will do a poor performance in the forthcoming contest.

21. *Very confident.* The athlete is sure that he/she will be able to perform at least to expectations. He/she also feels that there is a good chance of performing even better than expected.

22. *Can't take the competition seriously.* The athlete is not able to concentrate on the forthcoming event. It is

hard to get ready or even be serious about preparing for it. The athlete does not care about the contest result.

23. *Frightened.* The athlete is afraid of the experiences that will occur in the forthcoming contest. He/she has some hesitancy about competing. It would be nice to be able to withdraw from the situation at the time of completing the checklist.

24. *Other (describe).* Indicate any other feelings or sensations, for example, a health problem, an emotional problem, which have not been described above but are bothering the athlete at this time.

Excitedness Scale
The athlete should place an 'X' on the line which indicates the amount of excitedness that he/she is experiencing. He/she should consider the two extremes, imagine what they would feel like, appraise how he/she feels normally, and then decide where to place an 'X' in light of how he/she feels at that time.

Estimation of Winning
The athlete should place an 'X' on the line which indicates his/her assessment of the chances of winning.

After the Contest
Indicate the contest result and rate your performance as one of the categories indicated.

Pre-competition Psychological Checklist

Name_____   Date _____

Event_____

If any of the following descriptions apply to you as you feel now mark them 'yes'. If not, then answer 'no'. Complete this form before you see your coach prior to the contest.

	YES	NO
1. Can't be bothered attitude	____	____
2. Drowsy, sleepy feeling	____	____
3. Feeling of being alone	____	____
4. Feeling of weakness	____	____
5. Inadequate attention to preparation	____	____
6. Impatient feeling	____	____
7. Aggressive feeling towards others	____	____
8. I have cried a little	____	____
9. Some shaking and trembling	____	____
10. Poor movement coordination	____	____
11. Trouble seeing and remembering	____	____
12. I have vomited	____	____
13. I have diarrhea	____	____
14. I have urinated several times	____	____
15. I have had frequent bowel movements	____	____
16. Nervous	____	____
17. Butterflies in the stomach	____	____
18. Lack of confidence	____	____
19. Do not feel well	____	____
20. I do not think that I will be able to perform well .	____	____
21. Very confident	____	____
22. Can't take the competition seriously	____	____
23. Frightened	____	____
24. Other (describe)	____	____

_____

TOTAL NUMBER OF EACH   ____ ____

Excitedness Scale

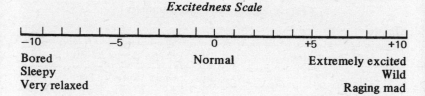

Bored	Normal	Extremely excited
Sleepy		Wild
Very relaxed		Raging mad

Estimation of Winning

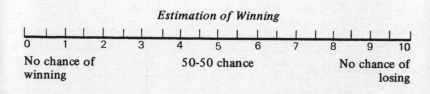

No chance of	50-50 chance	No chance of
winning		losing

Event or game result

Rate how you performed:

Great ___ Good ___ Normal ___ Poor ___ Very poor ___

Psychological Checklist Summary

Athlete: _____

Diagnostic	Performance Rating				
	Great	Good	Normal	Poor	V. poor
1. Can't be bothered.					
2. Drowsy, sleepy.					
3. Feels alone.					
4. Feels weak.					
5. Inadequate preparation.					
6. Impatient.					
7. Aggressive feelings.					
8. Cried.					
9. Shaking, trembling.					
10. Poor coordination.					
11. Trouble seeing, remembering.					
12. Vomited.					
13. Diarrhea.					
14. Urinated frequently.					
15. Frequent bowel movements.					
16. Nervous.					
17. Butterflies.					
18. Lack of confidence.					
19. Did not feel well.					
20. Thinks will not perform well.					
21. Very confident.					
22. Can't be serious.					
23. Frightened.					

Arousal Summary Sheet

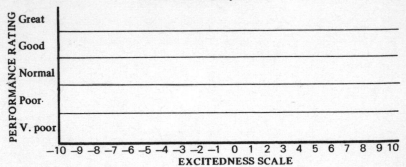

Sample Strategies

Example 1
The following example is a segment of the pre-competition strategy for activity at the competition site. The subject was a 15 year old male nationally ranked swimmer preparing for the 1976 Olympic Games Swimming Trials for Canada. A personal best time was recorded in the event at the trials.

Strategy Planning Sheet

Behaviour Description	Problem & Coping Response	Feelings & Appearance	Result
WARM-UP Before entering water swing each arm around freely, finding areas of stiffness	if very stiff stretch arms by swinging them around, front-wards, and backwards, pulling elbows behind head and pulling straight arms behind head—touch toes	no stiffness loose	
dive in and swim a relaxed 200 m free working on stroke and just loosening shoulders	if arms are still stiff after 200 m just throw them around and pull against areas of stiffness	200 free—stretched out, alert but calm	
pull 100 easy then 4 x 100 free pull on 1:40 ascending set	if pulls feel drowsy pick them up harder with burst on last length almost all-out still working on arms under body and pulling right back	pull—strong, easy fast arms but controlled; 100 effort—strong, fast—winded but not tired—could go faster	
another 100 free pull checking arms under body pulling right back, pushing in without stopping	as above	as above	
200 m one arm backstroke			
3 or 4 x 100 m free on 1:30 hard-race pace or better descending	if arms are heavy do a 200 m pull building up first 3 x 50 with last 50 easy	arms really loose; good feel of water	

100 easy loosen-up 200 kick at medium pace		kick: easy, loose; relaxed, alert	
50 sprint free timed	if 50 is slow swim back for another one then do 200 or more easy if needed	50 – all out stroke strong but not rushed	26.0±2
200 easy throwing arms around making sure joints are loose then six times without goggles	if still feeling stiff ask coach for rub	easy, loose, ready, calm	
BEFORE COMPETITION warm shower after warm-up; dress warmly (two T-shirts); sit with team	if any stiffness do partner stretching for areas involved; if drowsiness occurs think alert and do exercises	alert, strong, awake, NOT DROWSY	
once every ten minutes: – walk around pull – wild arm and leg stretching – rehearse race once	think alert; splash eyes and face with cool water		
10 minutes before race see Mr Talbot; rehearse; to martialling area; rehearse while stretching and bouncing; think mad and tough	to get concentration rehearse first 50 when stretching; read race strategy and say it aloud quietly	getting edgy, constant movement, building to mad and tough	
go to blocks; work arms and body; pump-up mad	close eyes and swing a mad first 10 strokes rehearsal	hard to hold back – mad as hell	

Example 2
An example of the section of a pre-competition strategy for activities prior to going to the competition venue. The athlete was a male world-ranked Canadian swimmer.

Strategy Planning Sheet

Behaviour Description	Problem & Coping Response	Feelings & Appearance	Result
wake-up . . . smile 'how feel?'	take extra 15 mins in bed; think about last summer		7-7:30
out of bed—check weather . . . sit in sun, feel warmth, good	if no good, do light stretching		
see what others are doing			
go to breakfast—cereal, juice, banana			8:00
stretching for 5 mins	do again if not feel right		
5 minute sauna then shave— get Bill or George to help			
work on correspondence course for 90 minutes	if can't concentrate then stroll around motel		10:00
see what others are doing	if not watch TV or play guitar		
11:30 see coach	else go over strategy		11:30
11:50 check equipment			
12:00 liquid meal; leave for pool			

Example 3

A sample of a competition strategy for a 200 metre butterfly swim. The subject was a 16 year old female swimmer preparing for the 1976 Olympic Games Swimming Trials in Canada. This athlete had little chance of making the team. Her best time prior to this race was 2:24.0. Her goal time was 2:19.0+. Her race time was 2:20.9 placing her sixth in the event.

This is a reasonably good example of a first effort at developing a strategy.

Strategy Planning Sheet

Behaviour Description	Problem & Coping Response	Feelings & Appearance	Result
200 Fly – 4 x 50 segments Behind the blocks look at a spot at the other end of the pool. Rehearse first strokes of race. Shake arms and legs, deep breaths. Mount block still thinking of first section.	Think harder and in more detail about race. Ignore everyone else.	Should be nervous and jumpy. Think hard of first section. Ready to go. Confident. On blocks thinking only of first part of race.	
On command think 'explode, blast, lunge'. Kick, pull hard. 'Speed, relaxed'. Are my arms pulling back? Push through, push through. My breathing timing early. 'Speed, relaxed, strong'. Are my legs kicking? 'Feels good'.	If I don't feel too good pull and kick harder for four strokes to pick up – then keep loose. Get more dolphin action. Breathe later.	Should feel speed, smoothness in water. Feel relaxed but excited. Check where I am.	
Check if turn will be hit right. Speed up into turn. Check position at turn. Turn 'blast, shoot'. Kick, pull hard.	Pull longer in hard strokes to get to wall.	Check where I am on shoot out of turn. After turn I should still feel good.	Should be up with everyone. 32.0+

Behaviour Description	Problem & Coping Response	Feelings & Appearance	Result
2nd 50 m Breathing, timing. 'Strong, relaxed' 'Kick even' 'Pull back, round out' Breathe late every two strokes. Make sure turn will be hit right. Pull harder, breathe late. Turn 'fast, blast, shoot' Gun-out of turn pull-kick.	If I am behind catch up over next 75 m. Even pacing to end of third 50. Swim as last 50. Long stroke, drive head forward, bigger 2nd kick.	At end feeling tired. Next lap is where I push through it.	With them
			35+
3rd 50 m Catch-up length. 'Fight, force, POWER' Kick hard, pull hard. Count 10 long pulls. Count 5 attack entries. Hit turn right. Last check point. 'Blast, fierce, fight' Big breath 'Drive' 'Bam'	They are hurting just as much as I am.	Shoulders tiring. Work hardest. It will be worth it.	35+

4th 50 m Head home, grit teeth. 'Fight, fierce' 'Smooth, hard kick, Smooth, hard pull. 5 times each.	Give it all. If I am behind, I can't panic; fight and go all out. Think cue words when it hurts most.	50 to go; be tougher than them.
Keep loose. Wall is coming. Put head down, go. 'Burst, lunge' 'Fight, fight' Kick, pull. Dive head for wall and kick.		As the wall comes fight to beat out another swimmer (real or imaginary) in the next lane. As I finish, I look at the clock to see my time, and a feeling of relief comes over me.
		36+ 2.19+

Example 4

A sample competition strategy for a 400 metre individual medley swim. The subject was a 16 year old male swimmer competing in the final of the event at the 1976 Olympic Games. The resulting time was a personal best performance.

This strategy examples segmenting the distance into 8 units. There is a scarcity of coping behaviours because this athlete preferred to swim 'his' race and not to care about the other swimmers. There is an abundance of mood words because they were deemed to be more helpful than concentrating on technique. No goal times were established because the athlete was more concerned with maximizing his effort. He would accept whatever time was achieved as long as the effort was the very best that he could produce. This strategy was the second one formed for serious competitions.

Strategy Planning Sheet

Behaviour Description	Problem & Coping Response	Feelings & Appearance	Result

400 IM
1) Stand behind block
  – stretch, keep warm
  – check equipment
2) Take stance on block
  – easy stretch and shake-out of legs and arms
  – take some deep breaths
  – think explosive thoughts
  – take off with the buzzer, releasing the prior tenseness
		Think positive, stay loose
		Confident
		
		Concentrate on what is going to happen in *your* lane
		Tense like a cat about to spring	

50 m Fly
Hit water
Kick good and hard and get going
Feel strong with speed in stroke
Feel power and drive from legs
Arms under body with powerful stroke
Think 'might, force, solid, propel'
Accelerate into turn
Think wall is untouchingly hot
	Stroke–watch timing
	  –late breathing
	  –watch timing
		Get to surface and get going
		Fly is 2 x 50 not 100 m
		Aggress into others
		Turn anger into useful energy
		Get off the wall as fast as possible	

Behaviour Description	Problem & Coping Response	Feelings & Appearance	Result
2nd 50 Fly Get to surface as quickly as possible 'Quick, power' 'Rap, jab, force' Drive forward Arms under Accelerate into turn Get off 'hot' wall quickly		feel strong and speed aggress others; use it forget what has happened concentrate on what lies ahead	
Back 3rd 50 m Surface quickly Kick Make sure you have hold of the water with arms Be strong and powerful— 'solid, powerful, might, blast, rapid, alert' Look for wall Hit 'hot' wall and get off it		must disregard sense of vision; think of race and do not lose concentration because of what vision picks up (crowd, timers, other swimmers) use aggressiveness towards others ahead lies 50 m back	

Kick like crazy to get to surface and on your way Think 'strength, power, quickness, CONFIDENCE Solid, heave, thrust, lunge, on-plan, good, okay, continue' Accelerate into turn Get off 'hot' wall	Finish arm pulls Don't roll body Get into good rhythm	At this point is very important to feel confident —feel that everything is okay and on-plan —best stroke is coming up
Breast 5th 50 m Take off wall with fast, strong underwater pull Immediately think thoughts of 'heave, might, explode, power, press, NOW, bold' Pretend you just dived in Accelerate into turn	Stroke —turn hands over —finish kick —drive forward	aggress towards others want to win electric shock feeling ahead lies my strong stroke my chance to take over lead and to win nothing has happened before breast
Breast 6th 50 m Wall hotter than ever—get off! —fast, long, strong underwater pull —power, press, confident —'smash, violent, thrust, crumble' —'push, be bold' —accelerate into turn		nothing but turning around and going . . . —feel energy revitalized and recognize it —50 m of breaststroke ahead —nothing else has happened —aggressive, violent feeling towards others —turn it into useful exploding energy —electric shock feeling (adrenaline)

Behaviour Description	Problem & Coping Response	Feelings & Appearance	Result
Free 7th 50 m Get off 'hot' wall surface quickly Force, confidence thoughts Crush, squash, smash, squeeze 10 metres out build-up Accelerate into turn	Stroke: arms under body pull right back	Get going as fast as possible —extremely violent thoughts but not going wild with stroke —want to get to that wall and blast away from everyone	
Free 8th 50 m Get off that wall and to the surface Get hold of water Think of nothing but blasting home Use crowd and opponents to increase desire to win 'Explode, rip, blast' Crash at the wall to finish	*Extra points* —if dead spots occur use aggressive feelings for support —think of water as being solid and water that resists you as being air or open space	want to win forget about body's discomfort	

Index